Dedicated to my grandsons, Stanley and Henry, and with grateful thanks to my daughter Victoria and son-in-law William and to our friend Gez Hughes for their assistance.

First published in the United Kingdom in 2022
by Over Bite Press.

www.bitepress.co.uk

ISBN 978-1-915292-39-1

Cover image by Will Finn
Design by Gerard Hughes
www.gerardhughes.co.uk

Printed and bound in the UK by Biddles, Castle House East
Winch Road, King's Lynn PE32 1SF

S.E.19

My London Life 1937-63:
An autobiographical and social history

Roger Ward

OVER BITE PRESS

Time

The time and place of one's birth and one's parentage are matters of fate rather than choice but in each case will powerfully influence, though not totally determine, one's future life. I was born on 16 September 1937 in a nursing home on Knight's Hill, West Norwood, a southern suburb of London. I was christened Roger John Ward, the middle name a genuflection to my paternal grandfather. My parents, living at the time in a maisonette in nearby Thurlestone Road, were named on my birth certificate as William Henry Ward, a printer's machine minder, and Winifred Beatrice Ward (how she hated the Beatrice) known in the family respectively as Bill and Win or Winnie. I was their second son, my brother Ian William Ward having been born on 16 May 1935.

Winnie, Ian and Roger

Was this a good time to be born? Few historians have had anything good to say about the 1930s. Literary figures – one thinks of T.S. Eliot (*The Wasteland*) and W.H. Auden ('*the years that the locusts have eaten*') – have savagely dismissed it as '*the devil's decade*'. Their dystopian vision was shaped by the Great Depression with which the decade began and the world crisis with which it ended. The Great Depression had destroyed staple industries and scarred the land with the scourge of unemployment, '*life on the dole*', especially in the heavy industrial regions of northern Britain. The war, the most destructive in Britain's long history, would result in untold suffering and upheaval, transforming the lives of my parents' and my generation. In between, however, the time of my brother's and my birth was something of an oasis, a calm between the storms. Unemployment was declining and a modest prosperity began to radiate through London and the south east, the region of our birth and residence, as new industries blossomed – the production of radios, washing machines, vacuum cleaners and in the Midlands cars. Cars were beyond the purchasing power of the great majority of the working class but the new domestic products were beginning to ease the drudgery which was the common lot of the housewife. Wash day Monday remains vivid in my memory as a day of damp misery in my early years. In all, it was not unreasonable to look to the future with optimisim.

Britain was at the time a stable, low crime, class differentiated society in which hierarchy was largely accepted and the privileged position of a ruling elite, deriving from heredity and/or commercial wealth and success, was held in place by deference. At its apex stood the monarchy, which survived the crisis of Edward VIII's abdication in 1936 thanks to the astute management of the King's 'Great Matter' by the Prime Minister, the avuncular Stanley Baldwin, who saw off Mrs. Wallis Simpson. Baldwin retired in a blaze of good feeling in May 1937, handing Number 10 over to the far more activist and abrasive Neville Chamberlain, the dominant figure in British politics in the 1930s. Far less socially appealing than 'the Worcestershire lad', Chamberlain, a scion of Birmingham business, nevertheless had a creditable record in domestic politics as a former

Minister of Health and Chancellor of the Exchequer. Under Neville, the public expected a more vigorous and competent regime than that of the ruminative Baldwin. Unfortunately Neville, a Prime Minister well qualified in domestic affairs, would be overwhelmed by the developing world crisis for which the nation was badly under-prepared materially and psychologically.

The threat was triple-barrelled. Three 'have-not' powers challenging a status quo which had left them with an agenda of bitter resentments: Germany raging against the humiliation and the amputations of the Treaty of Versailles; Italy because it felt deprived of its rightful gains from participation in the Allied coalition, in spite of having to be rescued by the British and French armies after its disaster at the hands of the Austrians in the battle of Caporetto; Japan because it coveted an empire in the Pacific necessary to repair its resource deficit with China and the decadent European empires standing in its path. The sleepy old British lion, lulled by the largest pacifist movement in Europe, obstinately declined to look these issues squarely in the face. Hitler, burning with racist hatreds, was too easily perceived as a pantomime villain, Chaplinesque in his hysterical oratorical rants at rallies worthy of Hollywood staging. Surely this was political theatre?

Germany was far too sophisticated to fall for such crude demagoguery. In any case the British Empire was not in his sights but rather those Commies to the east blocking his lebensraum. Who could take Mussolini seriously? A posturing, pouting operatic performer posing as an ersatz Caesar. The vicious depredations of Japanese forces in Manchuria and China were well publicised but surely those stumpy and short-sighted Japanese soldiers would find Europeans a different proposition. While the wicked deeds of these aggressive countries were conveyed weekly to the cinema-going British public by Pathé and British Movietone News, accompanied by a plummy commentary and a dramatic musical score, appropriate lessons were not drawn. Little was done to update Britain's essentially colonial police force of an army. The great British navy – the essential foundation of our huge and scattered Empire – had been reduced to equality with the USA and obliged by treaties to accept the existence of considerable German and Japanese fleets. The Royal Air Force barely emerging from its sporting traditions to become a small but formidable fighting force. France was in political turmoil and the USA, grungily suspicious of the British, turned its back on international politics to cultivate its own selfish concerns. What could our parents make of this potential maelstrom? With trenches being dug in Hyde Park in September 1938 Europe seemed to be on the brink of war. Fears were about to be turned into realities but good old Neville came up with a saving solution, leaving, it must be

THE JAW IS THE JAW OF MUSSO. BUT——

admitted, our honour a bit tarnished but anything was better than a war. The Munich Treaty, signed at about the time of my first birthday, was met with a hysterical outburst of relief. But, by the time of my second birthday in September 1939, Neville the Peacemaker had declared war on Germany.

In March 1939 Hitler had contemptuously broken the Munich agreement to occupy the rump of Czechoslovakia while Kristalnacht, the vicious pogrom against German Jews, administered a moral shock to the British public, demonstrating that Hitler's genocidal anti-Jewish and anti-Slav ideology was not mere rhetoric. A chastened and unprepared Britain found itself, against all inclinations, at war with Germany, with Italy

and Japan to follow. One can only imagine the feelings of my parents'
generation facing Armageddon, their world turned upside down. A good
time to be born? In a recent book, Selina Todd graphically describes this as
'the precarious generation'.

Place

West Norwood is an unpretentious suburb of south London, some five miles from the centre as the crow flies. However workaday, its inhabitants were Londoners and this was a great source of pride. No longer the largest city in the world, London still had pretensions to being the greatest. It was, after all, the capital city of the largest Empire in world history which was still, however perilously, intact in the 1930s.

It was the world's greatest entrepot, ships from every corner of the world crowding daily into its great dock complex, soon to become a prime target of the Luftwaffe. Not only was it one of the two greatest financial centres in the world, the other being New York, it was less well known as the nation's prime manufacturing centre, more diversified than in the regions. London was also, of course, the seat of government and a cultural centre to rival any in the world, its iconic buildings recognisable in any gazetteer or calendar. London pride was not merely a flower or a beer brewed in Chiswick, it was bred in the blood and bone of every Londoner regardless of status. Largely unspoken, it did not depend on usage and acquaintance with London's rich facilities. It was enough that they were there. I have few memories of family outings to any of the city's cultural gems, that would come later through my grammar school and through personal initiatives. Although I have lived more than two-thirds of my life elsewhere, it is hard not to feel a Londoner at heart, the links maintained until recent years through family connections. In the year of my birth London was still at or near the peak of its glory. Not yet one with Nineveh and Tyre, though inklings of the dangers in which it stood had begun to permeate. 'The bomber will always get through,' mused Stanley Baldwin and the fate of Guernica in the Basque country in Spain at the hands of the German Condor Legion in the year of my birth were an ominous and tragic illustration of his point. It is inconceivable that such dark thoughts did not enter the heads of my parents' generation, though too many of those heads would remain buried in the sand.

Norwood was located well south of the Thames and like much of south London had in development terms lagged behind northern suburbs. The Thames had acted as a barrier and there were possibly geological reasons for the paucity of bridges and good communications which accounted for the lag. To this day south London suffers from generally inferior connections to the centre, whether by road, rail or underground. Ask any visiting football fan which is their least favourite ground and Selhurst Park in south Norwood will figure at or near the top of the list. It was in the north that the most gentrified suburbs emerged, such as Islington, Highgate and Hampstead. There were, however, tongues of gentrification to the south. The Dukes of Bedford acquired extensive lands in Streatham and sold an estate to a wealthy brewing family, the Thrales, where in the eighteenth century the socialite Hester Thrales presided over a fashionable salon which attracted literary figures such as Dr. Johnson and Oliver Goldsmith and artists such as Joshua Reynolds. Clapham became home to the eponymous evangelical sect whose members included William Wilberforce MP, leading anti-slaver, Lord Macaulay the celebrated historian and Henry Thornton, a banker who gave his name to a local grammar school with whose alumni I would engage in combat on the football field on Saturday mornings (one of that corpus of London grammars since sadly abolished). One distinguished late eighteenth century aristocrat, Lord Chancellor Thurlow, ventured as far south as Tulse Hill, purchasing a thousand-acre estate and giving his name to Thurlow Park Road linking Tulse Hill to West Norwood, presumably for speculative reasons since he never lived in the area. The West Norwood cemetery with its many interesting gravestones and memorials was created on land purchased from Lord Thurlow's estate.

In the course of the next century gentrification stealthily crept south. The Chamberlain family, cordwainers of Milk Street in the City, moved to

Camberwell where Joseph Chamberlain, future Minister for Empire, was born in 1836. Ten years later they moved to Islington, to 'Highbury', the name Chamberlain gave to his great house on the outskirts of Birmingham built for him in 1879. By that time the Chamberlains had abandoned shoes for screws and once it was apparent that Nettlefold and Chamberlain was a success, the whole family moved to Birmingham in the 1860s. But the lure of London remained strong. In the days of his political prominence Chamberlain purchased a house in South Kensington. Although both sons, Austen and Neville were born in Birmingham, Austen ceased to live there after becoming Chancellor of the Exchequer in 1903 and, following his father's death in 1914, sold the grounds of the Highbury estate and passed the house in trust to the City of Birmingham. When he died in 1937 he was living in a mansion flat on Egerton Terrace SW3. Joseph Chamberlain's American third wife never cared for Birmingham, much preferring London and, while Neville put down much deeper roots, towards the end of his career he had leased his Birmingham house, 'Westbourne', and that city saw little of him. As Prime Minister from 1937-1940 he lived at 10 Downing Street and hugely appreciated the use of Chequers. The pull of the capital and not merely for politicians so often proved irresistible. The Chamberlain family were not the only ones to appreciate the appeal of Camberwell. The poet Robert Browning and the writer and art critic John Ruskin lived there and extolled the beauty of the area to the south, Herne Hill, Dulwich and especially Norwood, praised by Ruskin for its sylvan and unspoiled setting:

The Norwood hills, partly rough with furze, partly wooded with birch and oak, partly in purge green bramble copse, rather steep pasture, rose with all the rustic loveliness of Surrey and Kent.

Just south of Denmark Hill the road divides and one fork plunges down to Dulwich, rapidly becoming by the 1860s the most fashionable south London suburb (many years later to be graced by the retiring Prime Minister Lady Thatcher, though retiring is not a word which comes easily to mind in the case of that redoubtable lady). Since much of Dulwich was owned by a single ground landlord, Alleyn's Trust, its salubrious character was preserved. Land sold to the railway financed the fine buildings of one of Britain's leading public schools, Dulwich College. Among famous and infamous alumni who come to mind are Raymond Chandler, Eric Joyce (Lord Haw-Haw, hung for treason in 1946) and Nigel Farage! By the end of the 19th century gentrification was lapping Dulwich to reach my birthplace of West Norwood. A huge incentive for movement to the area was not only its reasonable accessibility to central London but its relative freedom from the notorious smogs which so afflicted London in the latter decades of the century and indeed well into the 1950s. Norwood was, as the estate agents loudly proclaimed, 'the fresh air suburb.' The growing popularity of the area is attested to by the existence in West Norwood cemetery of the graves of some famous figures, Thomas Cubbitt, builder of large areas of London, Hiram Maxim, scourge of 'fuzzy-wuzzy' enemies of Empire, Baron de Reuter of press fame and a number of Greek shipping magnates seeking refuge from the Graeco-Turkish conflicts in the Aegean in this quiet but developing suburb of London.

From West Norwood the roads begin the climb to, appropriately named,

Upper Norwood. Maps of the 1820s show that the area was still densely wooded, as indeed did the splendid O.S map of 1863, recently re-published by the Charles Close Society. The woods had long been known as the haunt of gypsies, some living on the edge of the law, daring souls such as the diarist Samuel Pepys in the seventeenth century recording visits to the woods to have their fortunes told. The presence of the gypsies in the area is commemorated in street names – Gipsy Hill, Rommany Road and, I suspect, Roman Rise, to which our family moved after some years in nearby Durning Road. The census of 1821 numbered the local population at a mere 1400 souls, rising by the 1840s to twice that number. The greatest asset of the area was, of course, its trees and especially the oaks which had been a valuable resource for the navy since the days of Francis Drake. Norwood's trees, processed by the Croydon charcoal-burners, had also warmed London dwellings until displaced by coal, flowing in abundance from the mines of the north and north-east. It was this transition which created the noxious pea-soupers for which London became notorious and was hated by all but French painters. But it's an ill wind. Located high above the Thames valley's foggy bottom, Norwood with its reputation as the fresh-air suburb, attracted residents and 'staycationers' needing somewhere nearer than Bath or Cheltenham for short periods of respite. A guide book of the 1830s described Norwood as

a village situated on the outskirts of an extensive wood and long-famed for the salubrity of its air and the beauty of its surrounding scenery, with smiling villas and blooming flower gardens.

Two spas were developed to capitalise on these natural advantages, one in Sydenham and a more successful one on Beulah Hill. In 1831 the Duchess of Essex opened the Beulah Spa Gardens and was such a frequent visitor that she went on to build a house on nearby Central Hill. A variety of buildings for the spa were designed by Decimus Burton – refreshment rooms, a wigwam, reading rooms and other facilities including a hotel. There was also a camera obscura, an archery ground, spaces for dancing and for performances by a military band. Entrance fees were 1/- for a single visit, 2/6d on gala occasions and a family season ticket cost three guineas. The spa with its mineral springs was very popular for a time but the advent of a far greater attraction in the 1850s, the Crystal Palace, brought about its decline. It closed in 1856, the site was levelled and sold for housing. Only the Spa Hotel survived, catering for visitors to the new attraction and lasting until 1936 when it was pulled down to be replaced by a tavern which is mercifully still there.

The fashionability of the Beulah Spa, however short-lived, encouraged development in the immediate area including All Saints' Church, which was consecrated in 1829 but was soon needing extensions including a spire in 1841 and further expansion in 1863. A number of villa-lined roads sprouted off Church Road, the main road connecting the spa to the central area which also boasted a new hotel, the Queen's, which would shelter many prestigious guests. A second spike of development, Gipsy Hill, resulted from the arrival (at Gipsy Hill station) of the Southern Railway. A second imposing Anglican church, Christ Church, was consecrated in 1869. By that time, of course, Upper Norwood, a place which few people would have been able to locate on a map, had become world famous, not for its environmental qualities but because it had become the site of one of the architectural wonders of the world which would attract visitors numbered in millions – the Crystal Palace.

In 1850 a Royal Commission was appointed under the presidency of Prince Albert, husband of Queen Victoria, charged with organising an international exhibition of arts and manufactures. World-wide invitations received a positive response, resulting in the promise of some 14,000 exhibits, roughly divided between British and foreign. A site for the exhibition was chosen in Hyde Park and architects were invited to submit designs for a suitable building. However, none of the 245 submissions satisfied the Building Committee, whether on financial and/or aesthetic grounds. The Committee were rescued from their dilemma by Joseph Paxton, an architect best known as a designer of gardens and the manager of the Duke of Devonshire's estate at Chatsworth in Derbyshire and various other properties. While attending a Railway Board meeting Paxton drew a brief sketch of a proposed design. While little more than a doodle, to their credit committee members responded positively to what was a unique and unconventional proposal – a great steel and glass building, essentially a scaled-up version of the Great Conservatory which Paxton had erected at Chatsworth to house a giant lily. Paxton was given nine days to submit a finished plan which was accepted. Paxton's work of genius was dubbed by *Punch* the Crystal Palace. The Great Exhibition of 1851 proved to be a sensational success. Opened by Queen Victoria on 1 May, when it closed on 11 October it had attracted many millions of visitors both British and foreign, among the latter many famous figures. Exhibits ranged from the beautiful to the bizarre but the greatest exhibit of all was the building itself, a singular work of genius by one of the most eminent of all Victorians. The Great Exhibition was temporary but left a permanent mark on London, the

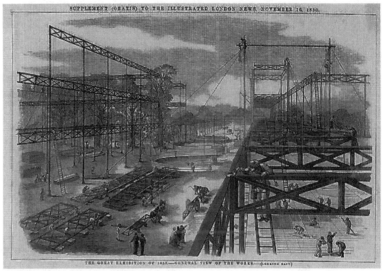

Early image of the Crystal Palace

profits invested in 'Albertville', the splendid complex of museums in South Kensington. When the Exhibition closed the plan was for the Birmingham manufacturers of the many tons of steelwork to dismantle the building and sell it for scrap. Determined to prevent his iconic building from suffering such an ignominious fate, Paxton, by then knighted, proceeded to form a company with a capital of half a million pounds to buy and resurrect the building on a 200-acre plot on one of the most elevated sites in London, the Sydenham Heights. There were doubts about the viability of a scheme located so far from central London and poorly served by existing communication. But Paxton, gardener, architect and also an entrepreneur involved in railway development, was able to ensure that the site was served by both a low-level and high-level railway, making rapid transit from central London possible. The recreated Crystal Palace was a revelation of Paxton's ambition: it was considerably larger than the original, five storeys instead of three and incorporating two towers designed by his friend and colleague Isambard Kingdom Brunel. As well as an additional architectural feature, the towers were functional, supplying the water which enabled Paxton to indulge his penchant for fountains, grottoes and the park lakes. The park also featured a maze, a race track and a great novelty, Professor Owen's life-sized collection of dinosaurs. In the belly of the iguanodon the directors of the company held a celebration dinner at the conclusion of which the professor delivered a lecture on geology from the mouth. Although little of the Crystal Palace remains the dinosaurs are still more or less intact, but sadly in need of restoration and no longer thought to be exact replicas of the extinct monsters. The park, of course, represents a fine legacy to south Londoners. The new building was no longer a mere exhibition centre, although the best of the original exhibits such as Osler's delicate crystal fountain were still displayed. It was to be a People's Palace, a scene of fun and festival – musical occasions for the highbrow, firework displays, military enactments and ballooning for the hoi polloi.

The new Crystal Palace was opened, like the old, by Queen Victoria on 10 June 1854 in a spectacular ceremony. The Queen was one of its greatest fans, returning many times and ensuring its fashionability. For the ensuing thirty years or so attendance averaged over two million per annum and included heads of state such as Napoleon III, Kaiser Wilhelm II and the Shah of Persia and many celebrities such as Garibaldi. It became customary for entrepreneurs to treat their workforce to a day's visit, as Joseph Chamberlain did on his retirement from Chamberlain and Nettlefold's Heath Mill works in Smethwick in 1876. Sir John Hardman, stained-glass manufacturer, also of Birmingham, complained to the directors of 'the utterly insufficient supply of first-class carriages'. Paxton himself bought a house, 'Rockhills', close to the Palace where he frequently entertained prestigious visitors and especially his patron and friend the Duke of Devonshire. The lavish style of the place, which had required a workforce of over 2,000 workmen to build and many hundreds to service and maintain, meant that it was never profitable. But Paxton who died at Rockhills in 1865 a wealthy man, had many other irons in the fire. This ex-agricultural labourer and gardener's boy had transformed a modest neighbourhood into a place of culture, show and entertainment known throughout the world. He deserves a far greater memorial than the giant bust still standing on a former terrace and a pub named after him at the bottom of Gipsy Hill.

The presence of the Crystal Palace meant steady growth for Upper Norwood, spaces between the villas filled in with shops and houses but mostly of a modest character. It never assumed the fashionability of a

The new Crystal Palace on Sydenham Heights

Highgate or an Islington since the great bulk of its visitors were day-trippers, though a few, including celebrities such as Wilhelm II and his son the Crown Prince Frederick and Florence Nightingale did grace the Queen's Hotel, built in 1854, with their presence. One of the most intriguing residents of the Queen's was Emile Zola, the French radical writer and journalist fleeing from arrest in France on account of his defence of Captain Alfred Dreyfus.

Unlike most visitors, Zola stayed for a lengthy period, eight months, in 1898, passing his time by writing and taking photographs in the area, still scenic enough to please visiting artists such as Camille Pisarro. Supposedly incognito, it seems that the world knew of Zola's presence and he received visits not only from his wife and mistress but from famous French politicians such as Jean Jaurès, later assassinated though not in Norwood, and George Clemenceau, later President of the French Republic and one of the Big Three at the Versailles Conference in 1919. Zola would later write nostalgically about his stay but at the time complained of ill-fitting windows and the poor quality of the menus. The Queen's still stands, popular for wedding receptions after ceremonies at nearby All Saints' church, my brother's in 1957 and later that of one of my nieces and a nephew. One of the legacies of the building of Crystal Palace was the creation of a workmen's settlement off Central Hill. Known as Newtown it gained a reputation for rowdiness and had to be surrounded by a wall. Something of this reputation lingered. Newtown was situated opposite to Roman Rise, my last address in London, and as children we always entered it warily on the way to the recreation ground beyond. Perhaps not entirely undeservedly because on one occasion I remember being punched on the nose by a National Service soldier on leave for the crime of engaging in conversation with a couple of the local girls. Newtown also contained the nearest pub and my father and my Uncle Reg would occasionally slip out for a pint on Friday evenings prior to their perennial card session. As far as I

The Queen's Hotel, at the time of Zola's stay

Zola at work

know they were never assaulted but perhaps they never attempted to chat up the local ladies.

Other than Newtown and, of course, the park, there was little left of the Crystal Palace other than memories and broken terraces by the time I was old enough to explore the neighbourhood. Even before the opening of the Great War in 1914, it had been in financial trouble. In 1911 it plunged into bankruptcy, initially bought by Lord Plymouth but then in 1913 by a Lord Mayor's Fund, in effect municipalised. During the war, somewhat bizarrely, it was occupied by the Royal Naval Division and subsequently by the Imperial War Museum before its move to Kennington. It experienced a brief revival between the wars but was finally destroyed on 30 November 1936 in the greatest fire that London had witnessed since 1666, the blaze visible as far away as Brighton.

All that remained was Brunel's towers and these were demolished in 1939 by government order for fear that they acted as landmarks for German bombers. Living a few hundred yards below the Sydenham ridge, the fall of the towers would have been clearly visible through the trees from our family home in Durning Road.

It may be family folklore that I watched from my mother's arms. During the war the site remained derelict and walled off. It inevitably aroused our curiosity as children and I recall sneaking through a gap in the fencing and gazing in wonder at the smashed statuary on the terraces. In those days parks were patrolled by brown-clad keepers (to us rather like Hitler's S.A.) and one needed to be ready to flee on the instant. Today, of course the

Crystal Palace on fire

Crystal Palace is synonymous with a somewhat inglorious football team which might have had a better future had it possessed a stadium on the site which had once hosted twenty Cup finals, the last in 1914 attended by a crowd of over seventy thousand including George V. Unfortunately Paxton has had no successors. Today that ridge, with the panoramic vista that Paxton made famous, at least hosts one landmark visible from many miles around, the Crystal Palace Transmitting Station, the eighth tallest structure in London. The loss of that iconic building stripped Norwood of its distinction. As a local historian wrote:

The destruction was complete, but a still greater damage was done to the district. Its very heart was torn out and the neighbourhood has never recovered from the loss of its centrepiece.

This, just before the Ward family arrived.

Uphill All the Way

My arrival in the world on 16 September 1937 was notable for a number of reasons. I was later told that my brother looked into my cot and decided 'He's all right', a compliment rarely to be repeated in subsequent decades. But he was essentially correct, his opinion validated by the judges in a Beautiful Baby competition sponsored by the *Croydon Advertiser* in which I was awarded first prize.

Prize baby

My mother's pleasure was tempered somewhat by the fact that the first prize was a silver cup (long since disposed of in the Birmingham Jewellery Quarter) while the second was a far more useful item, a pram of Rolls-Royce proportions fashionable in those days. But my parents also had a far more substantial reason for welcoming me into the family. I came not so much trailing clouds of glory as holding the key to a council house, for which the family now qualified. We were soon on the move to the newly-built Bloomhall Estate in Upper Norwood, where my parents would spend the rest of their lives. At about the same time an estate of private houses was under construction off Central Hill, adjacent to where my father's family had lived in Queen Mary Road. Apparently my grandfather offered to provide the deposit for a purchase but my father, an extremely cautious man, refused – the only one of the six Ward brothers never to own his own house. He preferred the security of a council tenancy to taking out a mortgage. However under-ambitious, his decision was not entirely illogical. The excessive inflation of house prices lay some years in the future and meanwhile a council tenancy was secure, backed by their repair and decorating services and at the time by no means socially undesirable and free from the stigma that would later attach to it. At that time less than 10% of working-class families were housed by municipalities and Lambeth Council was selective and expected houses and gardens to be well maintained.

As a recent historian wrote, council tenants were drawn from:

A relatively affluent working class, those in steady employment who could be reliably expected to pay its comparatively high rents.

My father certainly fitted this profile. He may have experienced some unemployment in his earlier days, which perhaps accounted for his innate caution and ongoing anticipation of 'a rainy day' to come, but he never in my lifetime experienced even the threat of unemployment. As a printer at *The Times* and at the end of his career working for the *Observer* and the *Mirror* group, he earned comfortably above the average wage. Printers were classed among 'the aristocrats of labour', the perishability of their product giving them, in my father's time, an unassailable bargaining position. Most of our neighbours were drawn from a similar social stratum, the 'respectable working class'. Along with their relatively secure economic status, they tended to live by a similar set of social mores, with 'respectability' high on the agenda. This context would leave an indelible mark on our upbringing and our values.

Whereas the majority of working-class families at that time lived in flats, maisonettes and multi-tenanted older premises, the Wards were moving into a brand new house on a brand new estate. Hardly a short straw. The estate was a credit to the Lambeth Borough Council. It was built on hilly terrain which precluded construction in straight lines. The 320 or so houses were built to follow the contours, in streets, squares and cul-de-sacs to avoid monotony. Most were of the non-parlour type decreed by Neville Chamberlain in his time as Minister of Health in the 1920s for which he was lambasted by critics for depriving tenants of that front room where children could do their homework, pianos could tinkle and courting couples find

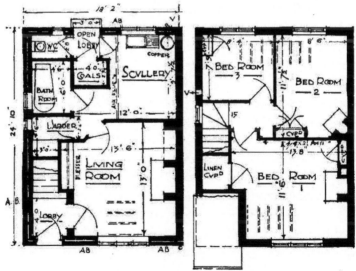

PLANS OF GROUND FLOOR AND FIRST FLOOR OF A.3 HOUSES (SEMI-DETACHED), ON BLOOMFIELD ESTATE, LAMBETH.

Plan for 3 bed semi on Bloomfield Estate

privacy. The sitting room or living room therefore was the most utilised, although the kitchen was large enough to be used for everyday dining as well as for cooking, laundry, etc. Off the kitchen was a bathroom and a large walk-in larder. The toilet was situated opposite the back door though easily incorporated into the house by the erection of an outside door, which was well within my father's DIY capabilities. Heating was provided by a stove in the living room with a back-boiler heating the water, later replaced by a tiled fireplace and an immersion heater in a tank in the kitchen. Upstairs were three bedrooms, two with an open fireplace which were never in use unless someone in the family was sick. There was a small garden at front and a larger one at rear divided into two parts by a concrete path, one side for a lawn and flower beds the other for vegetables.

At the bottom of the garden my father built a shed to house tools and bicycles and later a chicken run. A feature was an apple tree at the end of the garden which produced a prolific and maggoty crop of small green apples, the best of which would be wrapped in newspaper, boxed and stored in the loft for winter to emerge wrinkled and yellow. Like so many of the houses on the estate, our house (105 Durning Road) sloped from front to back. At the front it looked steeply up to the fence, the gate and the road beyond. At the rear it loomed over 'the Pan', a circular development with a planted area in the centre which would be a safe play area for us kids for years ahead. The downside for my father was the sitting room which was perpetually in semi-darkness and which, after long hours spent underground in the machine room at *The Times*, he found depressing. Some years later he would secure a transfer to Roman Rise a short distance away which was free from this drawback. These houses would shelter my brother and I as we grew up and would provide lifetime accommodation for my parents, my father dying in 1965, aged 63, and my mother in 1995, aged 89, by which time she had become a reluctant owner under the terms of Margaret Thatcher's right-to-buy legislation.

Some years later my father added to his garden patch an allotment situated in what was known to older inhabitants as French's Field, at the bottom of Gipsy Hill. Local folklore held that it had been a burial pit during the Great Plague of London in the 1660s and this, plus years of manuring by Farmer French's cows, made the soil very fertile. My father would set off with his home-made barrow at the weekends and I can still picture him sitting contentedly on his raised marrow bed smoking his Woodbines. French's Field was surely good for his mental and physical well-being but the Woodbines would contribute to his early death from lung cancer. His other addiction was to his chickens, which he reared during the post-war years of austerity. He had a peculiar affinity with his birds, which would follow him around the garden clucking happily. A hen called Betty would regularly wander into the house, clearly regarding herself as a member of the family. Another, a fierce cockerel, would attack anyone but my father who ventured down the garden. It broke his heart to kill his birds at Christmas time and the dread deed had to be performed by my uncle Sid, who had no such compunction. Father later transferred his affections to a budgerigar called Chippy, who faithfully reproduced my father's Cockney tones and would perch contentedly on his nose while he snoozed. Great was the lament when Chippy, his cage put out in the garden for an airing, burst out and refused all inducements to return, presumably meeting his death at the beaks of the sparrows he had been so keen to join in the trees.

Parents

My father and mother were married at St. Luke's Church, West Norwood, on 10 September 1932. The groom was aged 32, the bride 26. My father was employed by *The Times* as a printer, my mother as a compositor in the press office of local newspaper publishers, Truslove and Bray. As was a common custom in those days, she resigned on marriage. She often spoke kindly of Mr. Bray, her former boss and was well regarded in return, as evidenced by the prominent spread devoted to the wedding ceremony in the Norwood Press, where it was reported as 'very pretty' and taking place in the presence of 'a large and admiring public.' There were full descriptions of the bride and bridesmaid's 'raiment' and of the reception at the Stanley Halls in

In the height of fashion

South London, after which the couple departed for their honeymoon to Cliftonville, a resort near Margate on the Kent Coast. They settled for a time in West Norwood where my elder brother was born on 16 May 1935, christened Ian William, with me following two years and four months later to complete the family.

At first sight my parents were not particularly well matched. My mother was more intelligent than my father both cognitively and emotionally and would have by far the greater influence on my life. She was emotionally self-contained, bordering on shy, very conscious of her personal dignity and not given to shows of affection, at least until her grandchildren in the next generation broke through the reserve. But for those who got to know her she was a loyal and reliable friend and appreciated as such. She was a strict mother, insistent on good behaviour, politeness and correct

manners. Rules were made to be obeyed and were enforced almost always verbally but with the threat of the copper stick in the background. Respectability was central to her values. She regarded alcohol as an existential threat, no doubt a hangover from her own upbringing, and she was puritanical in matters of sex, largely unspoken but nevertheless leaving no room for doubt. She was very stoical. My birth had left her with a legacy of phlebitis and an ulcerated leg gave her pain for many years, requiring regular

Sitting on the fence

bathing and the application of assorted unguents and bandages. Doctor's visits, at five shillings a time before the advent of the NHS in the later 1940s, were kept to a minimum. I remember her wincing at every step when her phlebitis flared but she would insist on adhering to her customary domestic routines. She also suffered from eczema, suggestive of a sensitive temperament. 'Grin and bear it' was the order of the day and she expected the same of us when illness or injury struck.

My school attendance record was impeccable and it was useless to plead illness. I well recall the mantra 'you'll feel better when you get to school'. Strict but not restrictive. Once we had done any domestic chores required of us we were free to roam and spend our spare time as we pleased. Traffic in our area was minimal and the word paedophile unheard of. Her own pleasures were few. She enjoyed the radio, usually had a novel on the go, the occasional cinema visit and the even more occasional visit to the theatre which, unless it was music hall, would send my father to sleep almost before curtain-up. Otherwise the only pleasure they had in common was the Friday night card session with my Uncle Reg and a friend making up the four. Without feeling capable of assisting me with homework she took a quiet satisfaction in what I managed to achieve at school. She and not my father was the parent who attended school plays in which I figured and speech days if I was in receipt of a prize. But there was no open manifestation of pride, verbal or otherwise. Life in the 40s and 50s was still very hierarchical. The vast majority of working-class children went into manual or lower level clerical and administrative work. Whether consciously or not she felt it necessary to caution us against excessive ambition for fear of future disappointment. This reflected her own life experience but took no account of the social mobility that was opening up in the late 50s and 60s and, however well-meaning, was inappropriate for the post-war age. I well recall being brought down to earth whenever relating some feat or other, perhaps on the football field. 'I don't suppose you were any better than any of the other boys', she would say. Similarly, in retrospect I was ill-served by her rigid egalitarianism which she applied to our upbringing: her sons must in all possible circumstances be treated the same. This attitude disregarded the fact that my brother and I were from an early age diverging, developing different interests and aptitudes. This divergence, he more practical and me more contemplative, would indeed last our lifetimes.

Where my mother's misplaced egalitarianism most affected me may have been in the choice of secondary schools, where alternative possibilities mooted by my junior school headmaster were rejected. She was adamant that I should follow in the footsteps of my brother. Unsurprisingly our respective passages through our grammar school diverged as markedly as it did in most other aspects of our lives. Although she didn't always show it, however, I felt that she took a quiet pride in my academic progress and shielded me from my father's preference for me to leave school, if not, as in the case of my brother, to take up an apprenticeship at 15, at least to leave at 16 when most of my schoolmates did, only a minority staying on into the sixth-form. After her death I found a letter from my headmaster, clearly a response to one from her, thanking him for what the school had done for me. The letter said complimentary things about me and, true to form, she never showed it to me ('I don't

Doorstepping in Roman Rise

suppose you were any better than any of the other boys'). Nor would she ever have openly expressed her pride in the fact that I was the first member of the family to have attended a University, nor that I would eventually return to London to teach in a local grammar school. Her long widowhood (from 1965 to 1995), sad though it was, enabled her to spread her wings a little and do some of the things, such as taking package holidays abroad and exploring London, which she had been unable to do during my father's lifetime and perhaps also to loosen up emotionally in her relationships with her grandchildren.

To the end she enjoyed the strong support of my brother whose business was situated nearby in Upper Norwood and who remained devoted to her and more sporadic support from me from a hundred and odd miles distant, having left London in 1963. Hardworking, loyal and unassuming, unselfish and with decent values, she did her very best for us according to her lights.

My father was a man of simple habits. His identity was largely defined by his work status. He was a time-served man, a printing machine minder, proud of his skills and comfortable in the secure employment these guaranteed. The long hours of his working life were mostly spent in the bowels of the earth, operating a huge machine in the basement of *The Times* building in Fleet Street. The Times was, of course, the *doyen* of the British newspaper press and to work for Mr. Astor, and even occasionally to be acknowledged by him,

Merry widow with camel

was a matter of pride. Outside work and the domestic scene father had few discernible interests. He was a slow, conscientious and methodical worker, able to turn his skills to practical DIY tasks in home and garden and extending to the repair of shoes.

He was happiest in the garden and on his allotment, his affinity with chickens probably accounted for by his patient, measured approach to work. As a father, too, he was an amiable and unthreatening presence, leaving domestic management and the general upbringing of the children to his wife. I never on any occasion remember him punishing me in any way or even scolding me. His unassuming good nature made him popular with friends, workmates and family, some patronising him as 'Old Bill', a simple,

Handy man

easy-going man. He quietly revelled in this persona, inwardly satisfied that it was an underestimate but not an offensive or inconvenient one. Beyond work and the domestic scene he had no interests and no pretensions. He was indifferent to life's baubles and his own personal appearance. Late in life he did acquire a car, a Ford Popular, on which he lavished the same attention he had always applied to the machines he had tended for a living.

He looked for little in the way of recreation outside the home. On our annual week's holiday on the Kent or Sussex coast he would never swim but would amuse himself observing the antics of children on the beach or fat ladies paddling at the water's edge with their skirts tucked into their knickers. Simple pleasures. The odd visit to the pub with my uncle Reg, the Friday night card school and the odd game of darts marked the extent of his recreational activities. He was not illiterate and had a neat copper-plate hand, perhaps the only legacy of his schooling, impressive if one disregarded the syntax and spelling of the text. The Cockney absence of the letter 'H' rendered the alphabet a thing of twenty-five letters. His sole reading material was the *News Chronicle* and especially the financial pages, for he was preoccupied with the price of stocks and shares, an interest he had picked up after leaving school and working for a time 'on the broom' in a stockbroker's office. Regularly investing small sums, he managed to build a modest portfolio, protection against a rainy day, which he always anticipated. This sense of insecurity may have resulted from periods of unemployment before his apprenticeship in the printing industry.

There was much that was positive in my father's persona which would account for my mother's unambitious choice of husband. He was easy-going, amiable, reliable and importantly, sober. He offered security as a bread-winner. There was, however, a downside. Not merely his very limited outlook on life but a besetting preoccupation with money: he was mean. Not self-indulgently so, his one outstanding personal indulgence was cigarettes, the Weights and Woodbines which would terminate his life, but imposing on his family the same spartan rules he applied to himself. Getting money out of him beyond the obvious necessities was a Herculean task, my mother's resentment of his resistance to her felt needs manifested in periods of silence. As my own perceived needs mounted in adolescence, I came to feel the same resentment. Apart from school uniform and mandated kit, which for me was often second-hand, he was unwilling to shell out. Perhaps doing an early-morning paper round, delivering groceries for a local store and medicines for a local chemist, all of which expedients I resorted to, could be seen as a good preparation for life, but it inevitably took time out from leisure activities and impinged heavily on the time devoted to school work. Added to that was a clear sense that he failed to either understand or sympathise with the direction my school life was taking. My brother fitted into his conception of a desirable future. Like my father he was practical and materialist: alienated by our grammar school, he left to take up an apprenticeship in the printing industry aged fifteen, the one legacy that my father could guarantee. He failed to understand why I rejected a similar path. 'What good will Henry VIII do you?' he would enquire. All this implied that, from quite early in my teens, my father had become irrelevant to my life except as the family bread-winner. To do him justice, he never implied that I was any sort of burden, in spite of tension between us. My mother quietly acted as 'honest-broker' when things became tense and helped financially when she was able for a time to do part-time work in a small metal-processing company in West Norwood. The relationship between father and myself could perhaps be described in terms of co-existence.

Surviving Adolf

For the first two years of my existence the Ward family was settling into its new habitat in Durning Road. It is impossible to say when memory begins and whether early memories are simply constructs picked up from family folklore and things overheard. However, I do have fleeting impressions in my mind of an old gentleman comfortably ensconced in an armchair next to the stove attempting to read a newspaper with an importunate infant thrusting a book at him with the peremptory order 'weed it, weed it'. The old gentleman, at least, was no figment of my imagination because for a short time my paternal grandfather, John Ward, lived with us before moving into a nursing home where he died. I have a photograph of him in his later years and fancy that I resemble him more than any other family member, intriguing for reasons which will later become apparent.

Our settling-in period was shortly disturbed by that evil genius Adolf Hitler. The long-dreaded advent of war with Germany was declared by Neville Chamberlain on 3 September 1939 and announced to the world in a querulous and self-regarding speech. Since the destruction of Czechoslovakia back in March the government had been stepping up preparations in anticipation of an aerial bombardment and among these was a plan to evacuate children from major cities, with London expected to be the Luftwaffe's prime target. The mass evacuation, sometimes of whole schools and of young children and their mothers has been much studied by social historians as a key event of those early days of war and with particular stress on the shock-horror confrontation between comfortable middle England and families of the urban poor. My mother, brother and

Grandfather Ward

I scarcely fitted the latter category, being well-scrubbed and under firm parental hand. But since we were two small and potentially boisterous boys quite capable of kicking chunks out of any sitting room piano, we were eyed with suspicion by the good ladies of Worthing when lined up in the parish hall. Little girls were distinctly favoured. However, eventually a gallant lady called Mrs. Alice Valentine decided to take the risk. My mother, proud woman, felt the whole episode to be humiliating and akin to an Alabama slave market. Our hostess lived in a substantial house in Pevensey Road, Worthing, the fifty-two-year-old widow of a ship's captain. Like many of her class at that time she was well-heeled enough to employ a live-in domestic servant called Millie, one of whose duties was to bring the cat together with the breakfast tray to Mrs. Valentine's bedroom first thing in the morning. I'm sure our hostess had the best of intentions and deserves our gratitude but I'm equally sure that my mother felt most uncomfortable and on edge in case her offspring perpetrated some dreadful *faux pas*. Britain waited with bated breath for the onslaught from Goering's Luftwaffe but what followed was stalemate in the west while Hitler was busy destroying Poland, cruelly betrayed by Britain and France who, except at sea, merely watched and waited.

The rest of the year 1939 passed without the expected aerial assault. Chamberlain declared that 'Hitler had missed the bus', unwittingly giving the green light for families to return home to London. The Wards were in the vanguard of the exodus. In the spring of 1940 the 'Phoney' or 'Bore' War ended abruptly. Hitler invaded Norway, the British and French intervention proved a fiasco and on 10 May 1940 Neville Chamberlain resigned to be replaced as PM by Winston Churchill. A broken and tragic figure, Chamberlain died of stomach cancer in November, by which time France too had succumbed in a disastrous six-week campaign, the remnants of the British Expeditionary Force had been rescued from the beaches of Dunkirk and Britain braced itself for invasion, 'Operation Sealion'. The prelude, the aerial attack on Britain, became known as 'the Blitz' (short for Blitzkrieg, lightning war). Throughout that summer, battle raged in the skies above Britain, bringing terror, death and destruction. The turning point in the Battle of Britain is reckoned to have been reached on 15 September, just in time for my third birthday. No party for me but at least relief for the adults in that it had become apparent that the RAF had not been defeated and Britain had not buckled. Battle of Britain Day, as it was named, did not by any means mark the end of the Blitz, which continued sporadically but with less intensity while Hitler adjusted his strategy and prepared to turn east for a massive assault on Russia beginning on 22 June 1941.

'Operation Barbarossa' came as an enormous relief to the beleaguered Brits, not excluding the Ward family, which had survived the worst of the Blitz though not without relatively minor collateral damage. Roughly half of all the bombs expended on Britain in the course of the war fell on London leaving thousands of dead and injured and whole areas, and in particular Docklands and the City, devastated. While the iconic central parts of London were the main target, a number of factors ensured that German bombs were widely distributed. The bombers of the time were notoriously inaccurate and also with central areas vigorously defended, the German pilots had a strong incentive to veer away and drop their lethal loads on the peripheries of the city and especially on south London which was on their retreat route through Kent and back across the Channel. South London, therefore, saw a great deal of the action and earned the title 'Bomb Alley'. Given Upper Norwood's position high above London, it was the perfect grandstand from which to witness the spectacular nightly action. Although Chamberlain's government and Baldwin's before him have been bitterly condemned for failing to prepare the country for war, in certain respects this accusation was exaggerated; the expansion of the RAF and investment in radar being obvious exceptions.

From 1937 onwards important measures of civil defence had been instituted and notably a programme of shelter building. Shelters came in two versions. The Morrison, named after Herbert Morrison, London's most

Anderson Shelter

prominent politician, was an in-house structure erected in the main room and resembled an iron cage in which the family could sleep safely unless suffering a direct hit. The Anderson, named after Sir John Anderson, Home Secretary in Churchill's government, was a more elaborate affair. It was built in back gardens, dug a few feet into the ground, lined with concrete sides and topped with a corrugated iron roof on which turf, sand bags and any other reinforcement could be piled. The shelters were installed by municipal workers at a charge of £350 for those above a certain level of income but free for poorer families.

Wailing sirens would give warning of approaching enemy aircraft and were the signal for thousands of Londoners to abandon their blacked-out houses and to scramble through the narrow entrance into the candle-lit shelter. We, like other families, spent many nights in the Anderson, especially during 1940 and 1941. Dragged out of bed, wrapped in a blanket, heavy with sleep, the children would be carried or shepherded down the garden and into the relative safety of the shelter. After so many years, I can still conjure up the sense of the befuddlement that this

Morrison Shelter

experience induced. When at last the sirens sounded the All Clear it was safe to return indoors, though by that time we children would probably be asleep in the bunks and could be left until daybreak. For us many of the scenes of the Blitz were exciting and I do not recall any feelings of fear though we must have experienced this. The weaving patterns of aerial combat over London, collecting shrapnel and spent bullet cases on the streets next day, even spending nights in the shelter (though that novelty soon wore off with repetition) were exciting. But one can only imagine the extent of the anxiety suffered by the adults and especially the parents of young children. For them the Anderson shelter meant at best snatched periods of sleep to be followed by the imperative of work the next day, battling exhaustion on top of fear. Perhaps also spending hours fire-watching or helping salvage squads. I recall my father and my uncle Reg sallying out to help at the site of a bombing on one occasion, Dad with a brand-new shovel which was snatched away by a warden and never returned. For years neither forgotten nor forgiven. Both men were 'civvies' at the time but the Military Training Act of May 1939 made all males between the ages of 18 and 40 liable to conscription. Inevitably the call came. First for uncle Reg, a former regular with flying experience: he re-joined the RAF and, as a sergeant, served in the hazardous role of rear gunner in bombers, a 'Tail-end-Charlie'. Then for my father, also joining the RAF, as AC2 Ward (Aircraftsman Second Class) and spending the war as a member of a salvage squad on a bomber station in Lincolnshire. In addition to having to leave the family in blitzkrieg London he, like other men in secure employment, had to face a considerable loss of income. Lives cruelly turned upside down.

As it turned out my father was much safer on his bomber station in Lincolnshire than he would have been if he had remained at home with us. For many years after the war I recall that one of the blankets on my bed bore the label 'Lord Mayor's Fund' and I can only think that this was a souvenir of the occasion on which we were 'bombed out' as the phrase went, though 'blasted out' would be a more accurate description. What happened was that a bomb fell on houses in the next street reportedly killing seven people and causing considerable destruction. Bloomhall Road was at a slightly higher elevation than our road so that the worst of the blast hit our roof, though front windows and the front door were also caught in the blast. We crawled out of the shelter in the morning to a scene of damage. I recall a couple of older boys climbing into our loft and addressing the outside world through gaps in the roof. One of them pulled me up to join them which I found more frightening than the night's fireworks. The house was judged to be temporarily uninhabitable and awaited repair by Council workmen. Meanwhile we sought refuge with our grandparents who lived a mile or so away in Chapel Road, West Norwood. Mum collected up her valuables, such as they were, piled essential items into a pram and we set off across Norwood Park and along Elder Road to No. 41, the family HQ.

No. 41 was a large and gloomy Victorian tunnel-back, terraced but spacious inside, the house in which my mother and her siblings had been brought up. Chapel Road got its name from a Congregational chapel situated at the lower end of the road while at the upper end, opening on to Knight's Hill, stood a stone-built and formidable-looking educational institution looking more like a penitentiary than a place of learning. Opposite the house was a convenient row of shops, including a handily-placed sweet shop and a greengrocer. On the same side of the road as '41', a couple of hundred yards along, stood the Bricklayer's Arms ('the Brick') of which my grandfather was almost certainly a prime customer and my grandmother a familiar visitor.

My grandmother (Nanny) was resilient, imperturbable and street-wise, my grandfather a taciturn and formidable figure but rarely in evidence around the house. For much of my childhood '41' was our second home where anyone in the family would be welcomed without fuss and where family parties and gatherings would be held. It was literally open house, the key hanging on a piece of string and reachable through the letter-box. My Nanny knew everyone in the neighbourhood and everyone knew 'Mrs. B', including the local unlicensed bookie. How long we were in residence on this occasion I can't remember but 105 was patched up sufficiently to enable us to return, as it turned out, only briefly. The Blitz was easing somewhat although the Luftwaffe persisted with its night-time raids. My father being home on a '48' (a 48-hour pass) coincided with a particularly ferocious assault. He was thoroughly agitated and insisted that we should all return with him to the relative safety of Lincolnshire. Suitcases were packed and off we went. I have no recollection of the train journey but I do vaguely remember drinking tea in the NAAFI at my father's base at Grantham while we figured out where we would find somewhere to lay our heads. Our saviour this time was a young NAAFI girl of my father's acquaintance called Lily Lowe. Lily lived with her widowed mother, Clara Lowe, in Sussex Street, Cleethorpes. Her brother, Charlie, was at sea with the navy and an elder sister Emmy lived with her husband Jack and their small daughter Margaret in the same street, No 67. Jack, a rugged ex-boxer worked in Grimsby docks, a reserved occupation, as did many of the locals. I remember the bicycle pack exiting the street in the mornings and returning in the evenings. It was with Emmy and Jack that we found refuge, a few days becoming weeks and the weeks becoming months while we waited for the German assault on London to cease or at least to abate. Cleethorpes proved a very different experience from our brief stay in Worthing. My mother bonded with the Lowe women, especially Clara with whom she would correspond regularly for years after the war, but also with Emmy who was a kind and gentle hostess, still in her early twenties. Little Margaret found it harder to accept having two older 'brothers' thrust upon her but could usually be cajoled when 'mardy' with a penny bun from the grocer's shop at the far end of the street. I remember being sent there to ask for milk or some other necessity 'for the refugees' but, as it became clear that we were becoming a fixture, Mum registered with local shops for our rationed goods.

We soon felt very much at home. Sussex Street was lined on both sides with Victorian terraces, separated only by 'entries', with small yards behind. It was a typical working-class area, everybody knowing everybody else, and we mixed easily in the street with local children, albeit mocked for our cockney accents. The Lowes, like many of their neighbours, were an extended family. One of Clara's sons-in-law owned a delicatessen and a visit on Saturday mornings would be well rewarded with a chunk of black pudding or a slice of pork pie. Margaret had three older cousins, Sheila, Pauline and Brenda and this inevitably meant birthday parties – my first introduction to the opposite sex and the delights of kiss-chase. At weekends, if my father could scrounge a '36' or a '48', he would arrive on his regulation bicycle and I remember being frustrated in efforts to ride it by its unusually high crossbar. Above all, perhaps, there was no need for Anderson shelters and no unwelcome visits from the Luftwaffe, such a relief for our parents who were eternally grateful to the Lowe family. I may have been safe from Goering's Luftwaffe but it was in Sussex Street that I got my first war wound. I fell off a backyard shed and onto a tree stump which made a sizeable dent in my left leg just below the knee. I was treated in the local hospital, apparently an early beneficiary of a new antibiotic called penicillin. I still have the legacy, a jagged scar. I later added a second war wound, a cheek cut while playing on a wrecked car back in Norwood. Bombed out houses, gardens, wrecked vehicles etc. being the playground and playthings of those years. Settling happily into Cleethorpes meant being enrolled in the local primary school which, again, I remember as a pleasant experience.

My brother and I, sharp little cockneys, were a little in advance of the local kids and I remember being entrusted with the class book fund to be invested at a local stationer. I can't remember the title of my first purchase but the cover juxtaposed a knight and a rainbow. It was a cheerful classroom, untouched by the fear of falling bombs. Two things I recall – making unleavened bread (much credit due to our teacher who was no doubt left to clear up the mess) and hearty renditions of 'The Lincolnshire Poacher', several verses of which I retain. Inevitably, however, my mother longed to return to her own household and eventually it seemed safe to do so. Initially this meant returning to the family refuge in Chapel Road since the house, though repaired, needed considerable scrubbing and polishing to bring it back up to standard. With the Allied invasion of Normandy in June 1944 it appeared that the war was entering its final phase, with German cities now subjected to massive retaliation and the Russians closing in on Berlin from the east. German resistance was bolstered by Hitler's promise of new war-winning weapons, beginning with the world's first pilotless ballistic missile, the V1, to be followed by the more advanced V2. The V of course, stood for vengeance but these powerful weapons were known to us as flying bombs or doodlebugs. Between the first salvo on 8 September 1944 and the over-running of the Dutch launch sites by March 1945 an estimated 1300 rockets were fired at London, with Charing Cross used as the bull's eye. Desperate attempts by the RAF to locate and destroy the launch sites (the subject of a recent novel by Robert Harris) failed. V1s were vulnerable to interception by British fighter planes but the V2 was capable of reaching twice the speed of sound so no defence was possible. Truly a terror weapon.

Exhausted Londoners were once again the object of Hitler's venom. The six month barrage cost the lives of over 2,000 people, injured over 6,000 and caused more material damage than the earlier assaults by Dorniers and Heinkels. 20,000 houses were destroyed and more than half a million blast-damaged. Most of the rockets landed in central and east London and, as far as I recall, none fell in our district, the nearest being the V1 which hit Norwood cemetery destroying the Dissenters' chapel. Relief in March 1945 turned to jubilation in May with Hitler's suicide and Germany's surrender, prompting wild celebrations in the suburbs. The ladies of our estate laid on a party: trestle tables were erected in the Pan and cupboards were scraped bare to provide sandwiches, jellies, cakes and lemonade for the children. I did have a photo of the scene, taken from the end of our garden, with my brother and I looking up from our place at the table to face the camera, but it is now unfortunately missing. There was noisy music from a wonky loud-speaker, games and races and general jollity.

As a married man, based in the UK and with a job to return to, my father was soon 'demobbed', returning home to 'civvy street' in his blue conspicuously short in the leg demob suit, which would serve him for many years to come, and a mackintosh, tie and a hat which he never wore, all government issue. VE Day was celebrated as if it marked the end of the war, hence the bitterness of the men of 'the forgotten army' still engaged in fighting against the Japanese in the Pacific theatre. The war in the Pacific was brought to a dramatic and controversial end by the dropping of nuclear bombs, first on Hiroshima and then Nagasaki. This final horror induced a Japanese surrender. VJ Day came on 15 August, marked with a two-day holiday. Bacchanalian scenes were repeated in central London, with American servicemen conspicuous among the revellers, but there was no repeat of jam and jelly in the Pan. Peace brought relief from fear but little else. London was scarred and pock-marked, Londoners drab and exhausted and if there were hopes of a rapid improvement in standards of living these were soon dashed. In fact newly acquired British responsibilities for the starving Dutch and the Germans of the British zone in northern Germany would mean more belt-tightening, not less. Hopes that the USA would rescue the Brits from the worst effects of deprivation were soon dashed: Lend Lease was terminated on the day the war with Germany ended and John Maynard Keynes' efforts at negotiating an interest-free loan were rebuffed. Not only would the 'Age of Austerity' continue into the 1950s but the international scene remained one of turmoil and hardship

Celebrating VE day

for millions, while new conflicts were also brewing. Against this troubled background Brits set about picking up the threads of 'normal' life as best they could – 'make-do and mend' an appropriate motto.

The ending of the war in Europe posed questions about the continued existence of the Coalition government. There had been no general election since 1935 and many people felt that one was long overdue. Coalitions tend to coalesce best at the top and leading Labour Ministers such as Clement Attlee and Ernest Bevin were willing to continue to serve under Churchill at least until the Pacific war ended. Rank-and-file Labour supporters, however, dissented and the party conference meeting at Brighton voted to end the Coalition. Churchill resigned on behalf of the government but received the King's commission to continue without the Labour members pending a general election to be held on 4 July 1945. To the final scenes of the war was added the excitement of an election, the first in my lifetime. It was inevitably chaotic, so many people no longer domiciled at their previous addresses, millions of service men and women serving overseas: drawing up the electoral registers must have been a nightmare. The prevailing view in the press was that Churchill would win and again form a Conservative government: it seemed inconceivable that the gratitude felt towards the redoubtable old warrior would not translate into electoral victory. Shrewd observers, however, had taken note of the impact on public opinion of the Beveridge Report, which had received such an enthusiastic reception when published in 1942. Sir William Beveridge, who ironically failed to get elected in 1945, had denounced the Five Giants of Want, Disease, Ignorance, Squalor and Idleness and set in train the notion of a post-war welfare state, of which the likes of Attlee, Bevin, Morrison and Strachey seemed the more likely architects than Churchill and his acolytes, many of whom in popular opinion had presided over the bleakness, however exaggerated, of the 1930s. The fact that many Conservative candidates campaigned wearing their medal-bedecked uniforms unwittingly reinforced the notion that Churchill and war were inseparable. The old warhorse did his own cause no good with his tin-eared electioneering including notoriously suggesting that Socialist government would necessitate some kind of Gestapo. Anyone looking less like a Gestapo Gauleiter than Clement Attlee would have been hard to find.

Did my nearly 8-year-old self take an interest in this politicking? Yes he did. Like most members of the working class and trade unionists, my father was a life-long Labour voter, though by no means strident in his political opinions. His oft-repeated trade union mantra 'a fair day's work for a fair day's pay' always seemed to me eminently reasonable and does to this day. My mother, daughter of a ranking policeman, might not automatically have shared his Labour allegiance – my grandfather and my Nanny were both staunch Conservatives, as also I believe was her favourite brother Reg – but I never heard anything from her suggesting she was in any way tempted away from a preference for Labour. We were working class and living in a council house and that was that. It was in that political tradition that I grew up. During the July election I attended my first political meeting, together with my mother. It took place in the forecourt of a pub close to the West Norwood cemetery and was in support of Ronald Chamberlain (no relation to the famous family), who was seeking to unseat Duncan Sandys, Churchill's son-in-law, campaigning in the uniform of a Colonel of the General Staff. I recall children singing 'vote, vote, vote for Mr. Chamberlain. Kick old Sandys down the stairs' and no doubt I joined in. After the meeting my mother was enthusiastic enough to approach Chamberlain for his autograph and, for good measure, also his wife's. I later used her autograph book to collect the signatures of footballers.

The Norwood voters obliged and Ronald Chamberlain was sent to Westminster as one of Labour's 146 vote majority. The simple task of Attlee's government was to establish the 'new Jerusalem' in a shattered land struggling under a mountain of debt amid global turmoil and with a new international chasm already beginning to open up between the Western Powers and the Soviet Union, soon to be identified as 'the Cold War'. Not unreasonably David Kynaston, in his book *Austerity Britain* (2007) argues that the six years following the six years of war were 'in some ways even harder than the years of the war itself'. For housewives, shortages and rationing posed a daily problem, hopes of relief dashed when bread joined the lengthy list of rationed goods in 1946. The few items off the ration were voraciously hunted down, with queues quickly forming at a hint or a rumour of supply. Britons became a byword for forming orderly if less than cheerful queues. I remember resenting being sent to join the Saturday morning queue outside Kennedy's, a delicatessen in Upper Norwood High Street, to secure a pound of their excellent chipolatas. A day's menu solved.

Labour's big two

Coupons were as valued as banknotes and as scarce. The government made an effort to safeguard children, their green ration books, as opposed to the buff-coloured adult ones, guaranteeing extra supplies of milk and fruit. Concentrated orange juice from the US was sweet and palatable, the same could not be said of cod liver oil. As busy, active children we were always hungry and on the lookout for anything edible but, according to nutritionists, we were not ill-nourished. The notorious lack of culinary skills of the average British housewife didn't help matters and the end result was a generally stodgy, monotonous diet, short on protein but strong on root vegetables and greens. I do not exclude my mother from the accusation of lacking culinary imagination. She was very traditional in the kitchen and our menu very predictable. However, the task facing housewives was truly formidable and they deserved every sympathy. The same was true of the women working in school kitchens. I have never met anyone of my generation who has a favourable word to say for school dinners. My junior school, from age seven to ten, was near enough for me to run home at lunchtime. At secondary school the dinners seemed to me to be dire, with teachers policing the dining hall to ensure that they were eaten and not scraped into the bin. Pity the poor dinner ladies who had to battle daily with shortages and small budgets. My brother's dinners cost 5d a day and mine 4d, a very small sum even in those times. When I think of school dinners, memories of Mrs. Webber come to mind. At Tenison's Mrs. Webber's role was to dish out the puddings. She had taken a shine to me and when I reached her in the queue I would be greeted with a confidential smile and an extra portion of something uneatable. What else could I do but smile back and say 'thank you'? Dear Mrs. Webber…

With the best of intentions progress towards the new Jerusalem was glacial. It was a case of 'Starve with Strachey and shiver with Shinwell' (the Ministers responsible respectively for food and fuel) and the wags were soon beginning to question whether Britain had actually won the war. But for us children, who had never known 'the days of wine and roses' nostalgically conjured up by jaundiced adults, it was our daily reality and we didn't miss what we had never known. Returning to London meant, for my brother and I, attending St. Joseph's School on Central Hill which my father and his brothers had once attended. A Catholic primary and junior school, single storey, late Victorian and cottagey, it was only some ten minutes walk from our estate, fifteen if in dawdling mode. There were new friends to make at school and on the estate and a blitzed world to explore.

Family: the Wards

My father was born on 21 December 1902, christened William Henry and known to all as Bill. The fourth of six sons born to John and Mary Ward of Queen Mary Road, Upper Norwood, he had three elder brothers: Bernard (Bernie), born 1894, Jack born 1895 and Sid born 1899. After a gap of a decade came two more brothers, Harry born 1909 and Alfred born 1911, always known as Dick. A solitary daughter, christened Nellie and known to her brothers as 'Sis', died aged only 13. My grandfather (1866-1942) earned his living as a painter and decorator, family folklore crediting him with high-class work which included re-gilding the gates of Buckingham Palace. My grandmother (1870-1934) née Goldsmith, a name suggestive of a Jewish background, was always remembered by her sons with great affection. Every year on Christmas morning my father and my uncle Sid, the only brothers still living in the area, met to lay a wreath on the family grave in Streatham cemetery. My grandfather died in a nursing home amid the chaos of wartime in 1942. The only photograph I have of him shows a white-haired, white-moustached, well-dressed old gentleman to whom I feel I bear more resemblance than to anyone else in the family.

With him died a family mystery, which was investigated by the youngest of his sons, Dick, in retirement, when he was on the verge of emigrating to New Zealand, where he spent the rest of his life. For years my Ward uncles would joke about a possible Italian connection in the family but none had made any attempt before Dick to track it down. All the boys had attended St. Joseph's school, a Catholic primary school in Upper Norwood which was part of a large Catholic complex comprising a church, the Virgo Fidelis convent, a private girls' school and a Presbytery, all set in extensive woodlands stretching from Crown Dale to Central Hill known as the Convent Woods. The Ward family, in Queen Mary Road, was separated from this Catholic complex only by a field in which my father remembered donkeys grazing but which, by the 1930s, had been built over with pleasant middle-class housing. The Ward children had only to run the couple of hundred yards to the school and in the next generation my brother and I would do the same from the other direction. But were the Wards a Catholic family? Dick's enquiries at the Church and school drew a blank, many church and parish records, he was informed, had been destroyed or lost during the war. So there were no baptismal records and the only evidence of a Catholic connection was the marriage of my uncle Jack to his wife Lottie in 1917 in St. Joseph's church. Neither my father nor my mother were churchgoers and were certainly not Catholics. They had married in an Anglican church and did not bring up my brother and I as Catholics in any sense other than that we attended a Catholic primary school when most of the children on our estate went to the state primary in Gipsy Road. The Sunday school we attended as children was in the Methodist church in Upper Norwood, now the site of a Tesco. Yet census and other records suggest that my grandfather's origins were both Catholic and part Italian. His parents were Augustus and Helen Bolognese. Augustus was a waiter and Helen the daughter of a coachman called Mahoney, bringing a hint of Irish into the equation. They were married in Holborn in 1865 and in the next thirteen years produced seven children, of which my grandfather, christened John Bolognese, was the eldest. When he married Mary Goldsmith in 1893 he was recorded in the Register as John Ward Bolognese but by the time of the 1911 Census he had dropped the Bolognese. Where had the Ward name come from and why had he forsworn Bolognese? One possible explanation is that he may have been adopted by a family called Ward and taken their name. What about his numerous siblings? Here the church records were more helpful, revealing that there were Bologneses living in the Norwood area and several Bolognese christenings had taken place. These would have been cousins of the Ward boys but they could not remember ever having socialised with any Bologneses with the single exception of an Aunt Ada, who would have been their father's sister, who had clearly married well since my father remembered her visiting in a carriage. My father and Dick both remembered attending her funeral. Dick and my mother were most amused by what he had found out, partial though it was. For me the mystery was deepened by the fact that my grandfather did not look in the least Italian but that the Ward boys, dark-haired and inclined to be swarthy, did. The legacy of this mysterious connection for me was to attend a Catholic primary school as a non-Catholic following somewhat anonymously in the footsteps of my father and his brothers. There is a saying attributed to the Jesuits, 'give us the child and we will give you the man'. Many years later a colleague with whom I shared a study declared during one of our many discussions that I was imbued with Catholic theology. Perhaps, after all, my three years at St. Joseph's primary school had left its mark.

Of the six Ward brothers my father was markedly the least ambitious and the least upwardly mobile. The eldest, Bernie, suffered gassing while serving in the army in France and Belgium during the war of 1914-18 and died relatively young. I do not remember ever having met him though I do have warm memories of his widow, Auntie Flo, a feisty and cheerful little Yorkshire woman who revered his memory and would regale us with photographs on the rare occasions that we visited.

Bernie (seated), eldest of Ward bros, at war with the Kaiser

Her second husband, John, a retired builder, would sit by philosophically while she made it obvious that Bernie had been the love of her life. She had no children of her own but lived long enough to encounter mine. She lived in Tunbridge Wells and I remember our last meeting – an enjoyable visit to Sissinghurst. John, a gentle soul, once explained to me that he had retired because 'the mud had been sucking at my boots'. He died before Flo, thus she was twice widowed.

The next eldest was Jack, a Catholic at least at the time of his marriage but whether he remained a communicant I don't know. Jack became a printer and a 'father of the chapel' – a shop steward in the printing industry. My father looked up to him and it was almost certainly Jack who had secured his apprenticeship. Jack was an archetypal labour aristocrat and moderately prosperous. He and Lottie lived in a substantial house in West Wickham which, in the absence of a family car on either side, meant there were relatively few visits. They had no children but were always welcoming to my brother and I, even when we scalped their extensive lawn with their new mower. The house was furnished in what to me seemed a very plush and old-fashioned style. Jack died while I was still in my early teens and Lottie sold up and moved to Corfe Castle in Dorset, where she married again. Apart from the odd postcard, contact was lost.

The third of Dad's elder brothers was Sid, the only one to remain in the area and therefore the one that I got to know best and see most often. He was old enough to have served in the army in WW1 and had been sent to one of the more diversionary and pointless of allied expeditions, to Salonika in Greece. His only comment on this experience I can recall was that Greeks could steal the wheels off your bicycle while you were still on the move. Like so many of that generation Sid had been relieved to get back to Blighty in one piece and had no wish to ever venture abroad again. Years later, after a week's holiday in Austria, his sole reflection was that Austrians couldn't make a decent cup of tea. Any notion that this generation was guilty of chauvinism, imperial nostalgia or any kind of flag-waving is seriously wide of the mark. 'Little Englanders' would be a more accurate description if the evidence of my uncles is anything to go by. I was fond of Sid, genial and easy-going, I always received a friendly welcome at his printing works, situated in a yard behind a pub and opposite the public library in Upper Norwood.

The printing works were ramshackle and unheated except for a coke stove on which was placed a bowl of ink-stained water. Health and safety? Both floors were packed with machines, many of which were seldom in use. Sid's principal business was supplying posters and 'flyers' to local enterprises and community groups and texts for local churches. He tried to persuade my father to join him but that cautious man was not prepared to take that or any other chance. He was always scathing about Sid's slapdash methods, contrasting them with his own meticulous standards at The Times. It was probably a wise decision; he and Sid were chalk and cheese. Sid had one assistant, Maud, his compositor. She was a cheerful single woman living with her sisters Faith and Charity and like Sid was warm and friendly in spite of the spartan environment of the works. Sid was married to a Welsh lady, Gwladys, and she was usually cited as the reason the families didn't socialise more. She was always depicted as a woman of uncertain and very volatile temper, though I never experienced this side of her character myself. Their only son, my cousin Ken, was a few years older than my brother. Ken attended a private school, the Catholic St. Joseph's College (the Catholic connection again!) on Beulah Hill. Aspirations for him to become a doctor came to nothing and he ended up in the printing works with his father, where he always struck me as contented with his lot. He was a keen footballer, playing for a local team and later reached county-class at bowls. By my parents, Ken was often depicted as arrogant, 'a big head', a reflection no doubt of his private education, the 'tall poppy syndrome' regrettably at work but a perception not shared by me.

Sid's family lived at 45 Wright's Road, South Norwood, very close to the Crystal Palace football stadium, Selhurst Park. It was, and still is, one of the least pretentious of football grounds, shoe-horned in to an area of terraced houses and close-packed streets. I was interested in football on my own account but the connection with CPFC was deepened through my uncle. In those days of the maximum wage – Stanley Matthews once complained that the bandsmen at the Cup Final were paid more than he was – many footballers took lodgings in the vicinity of their clubs. Sid usually had a team member lodging with him. I remember one, a hulking Welsh full-back, belting out tunes on the front-room piano and also a winger called Ted Broughton (known on the terraces as Granny), who was kind enough to take my autograph book into the dressing rooms. I still have it: pages of the names of footballers plying their craft in the Third Division South of the Football League. The one famous name among them, inscribed on two separate occasions, was that of the great Tommy Lawton, ex-Chelsea and England and in the years after the war plying his trade with Notts County.

Selhurst Park

On match days I could easily spot my uncle, who sported a ginger-coloured fedora which marked him out in the crowd on the terrace at the Holmesdale Road end. Afterwards there would always be a cup of tea on offer in Wright's Road from my allegedly temperamental aunt Gwladys. One abiding memory I have is of Sid the chicken killer. For some years my father kept chickens but couldn't bear to despatch them. Sid had no such qualms – shades of Salonika? I remember the excitement as he pursued a feisty cockerel around the garden before finally cornering it and wringing its neck. My father had an amazing affinity with chickens and later with a budgerigar which could faithfully replicate his cockney tones. That feisty

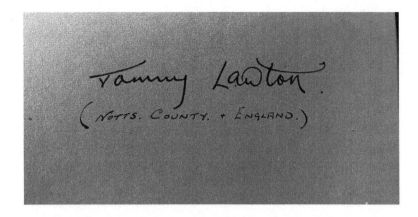

Tammy Lawton.
(NOTTS. COUNTY. + ENGLAND.)

cock would attack anyone going into the garden when he was loose who was not my father. For a time we had a hen called Betty who would follow him around clucking contentedly and would frequently wander into the house to enjoy a few tit-bits on a saucer, including ice-cream when available. Occasionally Betty would take a stroll down Durning Road to be brought back by a neighbour. My father couldn't bear to contemplate a violent death for Betty at the hands of my uncle and she was allowed to die of old age, by which time she was unpotable.

Dad's two youngest brothers, Harry and Dick, seemed to belong to a different generation. In dress, attitudes and lifestyle they offered a contrast to their older brothers, having been sheltered from life's struggles through the existence of the age gap. Harry had what was generally termed 'the gift of the gab': he was a natural salesman and enjoyed a successful career with an office machine company. He was married to Kath, a lady from Brighton and they eventually settled in Birmingham. Moving smoothly into the middle class, they lived in Birmingham's classier suburbs, Sutton Coldfield and then Wylde Green. They had one child, a daughter, Julia, who was sophisticated and vivacious and would entertain by singing and playing piano. Sometime after she had left school Harry set her up in a lingerie shop in Sutton Coldfield High Street, 'Julia's'. She married a man called Ted, whose family manufactured vats for the brewing industry but, sadly, the marriage didn't last. Because of the distance between us we saw little of Harry, Kath and Julia but when they did visit it was always exciting and a highlight would be a trip in Harry's company car, usually an Austin. In 1955, when I was undergoing basic training at RAF Hednesford on Cannock Chase, I was able to spend a weekend with them and experience Birmingham for the first time. Sadly, by the time I had moved to Birmingham myself in 1963, Julia had died of a heart defect. Before the decade was out Harry, too, had died of a heart condition and Kath moved back to Brighton to be near her family. But this was not the end of the Birmingham connection. Dick was also a great talker and an engaging personality. During WW2 he was the only member of the family to enlist in the army and was commissioned from the ranks. After the war he also became a salesman and followed Harry to Birmingham.

Dick had married a Norwood girl, Mary, and they had one son, Tony. For similar reasons of distance, we saw little of them, although Tony did live with us for a short time during the war until able to join his mother in Pulborough where she had a family connection. I saw a little more of Dick after he had retired from business to run a B&B in Nefyn in North Wales. He was always good company, engaging and challenging in conversation over a pint. Cousin Tony became a merchant seaman and eventually a ship's captain. He lived for a time with his wife Carole at Poulton-le-Fylde, near Blackpool, before moving his family to New Zealand and settling at Brown's Bay near Auckland. Dick and Mary sold up and followed them. By the time I was able to visit N.Z in the early 1980s Dick had died but Mary, a gentle and elegant lady, lived on for some years. Tony and Carole had two daughters, the eldest of whom died tragically in a motor-cycle accident. The younger, Amanda, inherited Mary's bungalow and married a man of Maori extraction.

Family: the Barkers

In contrast to the Wards, the Barkers mostly stayed closer to home and were consequently a far more close-knit family and able to share occasions such as birthdays and Christmases. My mother was the eldest of the five children born to Henry George Barker (born 1879), the son of a Battersea bootmaker, and Vivian Muriel Thorpe (born 1882), daughter of a shipping clerk and advertising agent from Plaistow. The pair, respectively known as Harry and Vi, were married in Islington on 20 May 1905.

Vivien Barker

Harry was by that time serving as a police constable in the Metropolitan Police Force, having previously served in the army during the South African War of 1899-1902. (His service medals for both are in my possession, having been given to me by my uncle Reg).

Grandfather Barker's service medals

My grandmother, always known to us as Nanny, once told me that she had first caught sight of Harry in full-dress uniform marching through the City as part of a recruitment drive. My mother was born on 27 April 1906 and christened Winifred Beatrice, names which she detested (especially Beatrice) and was always called Win or Winnie. Her birth was followed by Henry Reginald (Reg) in 1907, Sidney Charles in 1910, Doris Louise in 1912 and Vera May in 1916. A further daughter, Grace, died in infancy.

My grandfather progressed through the ranks to become an inspector and was transferred from Fulham to West Norwood. The family moved into a large rented terraced house at 41 Chapel Road, off Elder Road and adjacent to Gipsy Road with its convenient schools, which the children attended up to the age of fourteen. '41' remained the family HQ for many years, a place to repair to in times of trouble, especially during the war and immediate post-war years. The house itself was a gloomy Victorian tunnel-back. Its downstairs rooms were situated off a long, dark corridor with a tricky flight of stairs before one descended into the main living room. Beyond was a pokey kitchen and at the far end of the house a toilet accessed through the yard. There was no bathroom in those early years but hanging on an outside wall was a zinc bath which would come into its own on a Friday night, to be filled with water heated on the gas stove. A feature of the sitting room, which functioned also as a dining room, was a deep, walk-in cupboard which was periodically filled with coal by the local coal merchant Bob Dove, who would leave the inevitable trail of dust in the corridor. Coal supply in these years was a perennial source of complaint. Strictly rationed, it was of poor quality, each hundred weight (cwt) containing more than a fair share of dust and also bits of slate suggestive of Welsh origins, which would spit out of the grate leaving burn marks on the fireside mat and even mark adjacent bare legs. My father would sieve out the dust and mix it with cement powder in sugar boxes to make briquettes, which smouldered each side of the grate. Nanny seemed never to be troubled by supply problems, the explanation for which would have been her amicable relations with Bob Dove, whose premises and stable were just around the corner in Elder Road, their friendship doubtless lubricated over a pint or three in The Brick. Such petty peculation was a perennial source of gossip and complaint in those straitened times. The upstairs rooms were spacious and like the rest of the house, generally gloomy. '41' was open house to anyone who knew that the key was hung on a piece of string reachable through the letterbox. Far from a bijoux mansion then, but to the family a secure and familiar environment presided over by my grandmother, the other two occupants being my grandfather, rarely in evidence, and my bachelor uncle Reg. Nanny was down-to-earth, practical and unsentimental. Not physically affectionate though we never doubted that she cared for us in her fashion and we never felt unwelcome. Nanny was slight and wiry, a bundle of restless energy. Hard-working but determined to enjoy life, she relished the company of friends and neighbours in the nearby Bricklayer's Arms with her daily tipple of Guinness topped off with a whisky at bedtime. She enjoyed a flutter on the horses and was a good customer of the local unlicensed bookmaker, regardless

The Bricklayers Arms

of the fact that she was the wife of a retired police inspector. She knew everybody in the district and enjoyed exchanging gossip. She was a font of Victorian aphorisms, many of which have ever since echoed in my mind as a constant reminder of her. Her relations with my grandfather were cool and matter-of-fact; she kept house and ministered to him but otherwise there was little apparent rapport. It was my uncle Reg to whom she was devoted. Of her daughters, her youngest Vera most resembled her in looks and in the capacity to enjoy life. My mother, while recognising Nanny's good qualities, was always faintly disapproving of her, taking a somewhat puritanical view of her tippling and of her attachment to 'the Brick', where she served as a part-time barmaid after my grandfather died in 1948. While still at junior school, should I express boredom in the holidays, my mother would pack me off to '41' where an errand or two was worth sixpence to be invested in the sweet shop opposite and, if Reg was at home between his shifts as a bus driver, perhaps the bonus of an ice-cream. I remember both with nothing but affection. '41', that gloomy Victorian pile, while it stood, was my second home, the family citadel in good times and bad.

In contrast to my grandmother, my grandfather was a remote figure. Although I was ten in the year he died, I never felt that I got to know him. He was tall and imposing, gruff and taciturn. He spent much of his time in 'the Brick' and, when at home, alone in his study. There was an obvious coolness towards him on the part of his offspring and a hint that behind this lay an unspoken history of domestic violence, with Reg and Sid obliged to stand up to him in defence of their mother. Behind such tension was the all-too-familiar spectre of drink, an endemic problem in the Victorian and Edwardian police force, resulting in numerous dismissals. My grandfather's weakness in this respect would account for my mother's lifelong suspicion of alcohol. She was not a teetotaller nor did she expect my father to be but she plainly feared drink as a potential home-breaker and disapproved of any form of excess, making her attitude very clear to us as we grew up. She once told me the story of being hauled out of bed in the night to play the piano for her father and his mates after their late shift. Another story, quietly circulated, was that my grandfather had once been reduced to the ranks after insisting on inspecting a muster parade while obviously the worse for wear. Fortunately for my grandmother's pension he then worked his way back up to inspector. When grandfather died I heard from an uncle that he may have choked on a bottle of rum when in bed with a cold. If so, a not unfitting end. Much of the tension between grandfather and the family passed me by. I was certainly not in awe of him and in a tentative sort of way he would reach out to me from time to time, perhaps with small gifts from off his desk such as a broken propelling pencil. Grandfather Barker was largely irrelevant. '41' was about Nanny, Reg and the family dogs, prodigious tail-waggers, first Bill then Blackie.

Nanny's domestic life was organised around Reg who, as a bus-driver, worked irregular hours. As a cheerful and generous bachelor with a sense of fun, he was the family favourite, loved by all and especially by my mother who would quietly discuss all her problems with him on his frequent visits to Durning Road. He was a great walker and in his spare time he would take in Upper Norwood and return via a long detour to Dulwich. If ever a man deserved the tag 'salt of the earth' it was Reg.

Knight of the Road

Decent, honest, warm and utterly trustworthy. If he had a weakness
it was lack of ambition. He was content to drive his bus for decade after
decade, retiring at 70 with a totally unblemished record and having
eschewed any promotion. This undervalued his personal qualities but
left him patently at ease with himself. As a young man he had wanted to
follow his father into the MET but had been rejected because, although he
satisfied the height requirement, he was deemed underweight. Instead
he joined the RAF, serving for years in Iraq and India. He never spoke of
his experiences, the only evidence being pictures of deserts and camels
hanging in the living room of '41'. After serving his time he joined London
Transport as a bus driver and was conveniently based at West Norwood
garage on Knight's Hill, a stone's throw from Chapel Road. Living at home

he was both a support and protection for his mother. For a number of years he drove 137s from Crystal Palace parade into west London and back and, if we happened to be waiting at our Central Hill bus stop, we would look out for him, a solid figure behind the wheel often with an empty pipe in mouth. On the rare occasions we travelled on his bus, we did so free.

He usually formed close friendships with his conductors ('clippies') who were therefore on the fringe of the family and would recognise us. One who worked with him for years, Bert, became part of the regular Friday night card school at our house, a great source of enjoyment for the four players and with us boys taking a keen interest in proceedings. A distinguishing feature of Bert was the absence of teeth. Like so many of that generation he had artificial dentures, which in his case were usually dumped in his tool box. Bert had served in the Eighth Army in north Africa and Italy during the war. He was a man of few words but what I deduced from his cryptic remarks in answer to my questions was that the common view of the rankers like himself had been that the much-revered Field Marshal Montgomery was a twerp. When I relayed Bert's views many years later to a friend and neighbour who had been an artillery officer under Montgomery, he was shocked. That old class divide. Reg, of course, was promptly summoned back to the service when war broke out in 1939. He served as aircrew and I believe, though he would never talk about it, that he was a rear-gunner, a 'Tail-End Charlie', in Bomber Command. As well as not talking about his experiences, he never applied for the various campaign medals which were his due. He had no time for the flag-waving and medal-wearing of British Legion types, which he regarded as posturing. Modest to a fault.

Besides my mother, his other two sisters were also very attached to him so that when he married in late middle age they were, to say the least, taken aback and scented entrapment, not without some justification. The lady in question was Margaret Pascoe, elder daughter of Gilbert Pascoe, a retired textile merchant of Knight's Hill and his wife, an ex-alumna of Roedean. Margaret had been privately educated at Virgo Fidelis convent school (that Catholic connection again). She had worked on a farm as a

Land Girl during the war and afterwards for an insurance company and, like Reg, appeared to be permanently on the shelf (but unlike Reg, not contentedly so). Gilbert Pascoe, a large and domineering figure, had other ideas. He was a regular at 'the Brick' and knew Nanny and Reg well. Reg was persuaded to give Margaret driving lessons – a possibly hazardous undertaking given that she was somewhat cumbersome and none too quick on the uptake and soon he was drawn into helping her with her accounts and when she informed him that they were going to be married that pliable man was too gentlemanly to disappoint her. In the eyes of his sisters he had been trapped into a marriage he would never have chosen. The plot thickened. After they had married and Margaret had moved into '41', Gilbert Pascoe bought the house at auction for a knock-down price, adjusted to the fact that Nanny was a long-term sitting tenant. A few years later a nearby industrial company seeking expansion offered them the alternative of a pleasant 1930s house on Convent Hill, a distinct step-up from the beloved but antiquated family citadel. '41' was then demolished.

Pascoe had transferred the deeds of '41' to Margaret who was therefore the legal owner of their new residence. At Convent Hill Reg had a pleasant garden to cultivate and he transferred his lunchtime custom from the 'Brick' to the 'Conk' (the Conquering Hero on Beulah Hill, named in honour of Nelson).

The loser in all this change was Nanny, ageing, increasingly arthritic, who parted reluctantly from her familiar habitat and the company of her friends. Her predicament worsened when Reg and Margaret decided that her daughters should take their turn in looking after her. Doris, who was at the time in personal difficulties, was unable to help, so the onus devolved on my mother and on Vera. Of the two, Nanny was happier with Vera, then living in Beckenham, sociable and with no hang-ups about her little weaknesses, unlike my mother whose disapproval of drink was all too plain. The increasingly unhappy old lady lasted until 1976, dying at the age of 94. A positive aspect of these changes was that the marriage of Reg and Margaret proved a happy one. The sisters softened and Margaret settled well into the family. She was good-hearted, devoted to Reg, hospitable and party-loving. She even submitted to cards, though prone to preferring gossip to focusing on her calls. She died of heart failure a few years before Reg. By the time he died in 2003, aged 96 in a nursing home at Farnham, the house in Convent Hill had passed to the Pascoe family. I mastered my emotions sufficiently to deliver a eulogy at his funeral.

My mother's other brother, Sid, was another member of the family employed in the printing trade, working for many years for Letts, a firm best known for their popular range of diaries. Although by no means unsociable, he was more introverted than his siblings. Quiet, thoughtful and serious-minded, he seemed to hover on the edge of family gatherings. His wife, Rene, the adopted daughter of a local family, was warm, chatty and more emotional than her reserved husband. Their two sons, Colin and Howard, took after their father rather than their mother and could be painfully silent. Colin in particular, a regular visitor to Durning Road as he grew up, could drive my mother to distraction by his lack of conversation. Both boys passed the 11-plus exam, Colin going to the Strand school in Upper Tulse Hill and Howard to Battersea Grammar in Streatham. By the time he had reached the sixth-form he had to suffer the embarrassment of having his older cousin (me) joining the staff in 1961. Our paths rarely crossed, however, he being by nature introspective and a non-participator in school life. But beneath the shy exterior something unexpected and powerful was stirring. Howard would emerge as by far the most celebrated, or perhaps one should say the only celebrated member of the Ward-Barker clan. After studying English Literature at the recently-created University of Sussex and following up with an MA course in creative writing at York University, Howard set out on a career as a playwright. To earn one's living in this way was by no means an easy path to follow but, as far as I am aware, Howard never took any paid employment outside his writing. In consecutive years a Howard Barker play would appear like clockwork. His work divided the critics. He could expect favourable treatment in *The Guardian*, while an article in the *Daily Telegraph* in 1990 described him as 'the wild man of British theatre' and his work 'as enjoyable as a toothache'. His plays were well-regarded enough for a group of actors to form a special company to perform them, their chosen title of 'The Wrestling Company' a recognition that interpreting his plays was by no-means straightforward. He did not set out to be conventionally entertaining, his belief being that the purpose of theatre was not to entertain but to educate. A major theme of his work was state power, which he saw as deeply dystopian, as in an early play *The Hang of the Gaol*, the gaol being the deep state, oppressive, corrupt and menacing. It was very hard to reconcile my timid cousin with this rip-roaring anti-Establishment playwright, spewing out sex and violence. His mother, though proud of Howard's rising fame, was shocked by the content of his work. 'I don't know where he gets it from', she would say to me. The critic of *The Guardian* opined that his work reflected the childhood friction between his Stalinist father and Conservative mother, a view endorsed by Howard himself. To me, over-intellectualising. Sid was certainly left-wing but I never had reason to believe he was in any sense a Marxist while my auntie Rene was only a Conservative in so far as, while working as a tea-lady in the Houses of Parliament, she found Tory MPs (and especially Enoch Powell) more polite than Labour. My own theory is that his plays were the product of a shy and timid personality, which his mother had done nothing to counter, on the contrary she had over-protected him. He came to view the world outside his immediate domain as aggressive and dangerous.

For a time after the war his family occupied a 'prefab', a row of which were erected on the edge of Norwood Park. Beyond the family fence local boys (including me) played football and rough and tumbled. Colin and Howard stood apart from such goings-on, carefully swaddled, they would watch the adolescent anarchy from the safety of their garden. Whatever the origins of Howard's inspiration, he is greatly to be congratulated on his success, which extended beyond these shores into Europe and especially Scandinavia. On a visit to Dijon in France some years later I observed that a Howard Barker play was showing at the local theatre. Howard had become part of the European *avant-garde*. He married a very attractive girl, Sandra, whom he had met at York. Although they had a son, the marriage did not last. Sandra became embroiled in the feminist wave of the 1970s, joining the Greenham Common protests, perhaps a step too far even for her left-wing husband. Perhaps characteristically, Howard showed no desire to maintain family connections, in spite of the efforts of cousin Trevor to persuade him to join the odd reunion. The last time I was in contact with him was sometime in the 1980s when he invited me to see one of his plays running at the Warwick Arts Centre, after which contact was lost.

By the time Colin had left school to join Barclays Bank, the family had moved from their 'prefab' in Norwood Park to a new estate on the edge of Dulwich, built on land that had once been owned by the notorious traitor Lord Haw Haw (William Joyce), not the most distinguished alumnus of Dulwich College. Howard had surprised the family and Colin too proved he had hidden depths. He developed a penchant for horses and carriage driving, an unusual hobby to say the least for a lad from a south London working class family. When offered a chance to move to Johannesburg in South Africa, he took it and in time was able to acquire some land and to indulge his passions. The last time I saw him was in 1973 when he brought his South African wife to England to explore the possibilities of a return. It was a poor summer and his wife was less than impressed by the climate while Colin found the price of land prohibitive. The decision to stay in South Africa proved to be a road to eventual disaster. He and his wife divorced and Colin developed early Parkinson's disease. At Christmas time I would regularly visit his parents and, if Rene had received a phone call, I would sometimes provide a shoulder to cry on. Worse was to follow. It was reported that Colin had been attacked and injured, his Land Rover stolen. Soon after this tragic incident he died, still relatively young. The couple had a son whom regrettably I have never met.

My mother's sister Doris remained a Barker by dint of marrying a cousin, Cyril, from the Fulham branch of grandmother's family. Doris was a gentle, easy-going person, amiable and good company. Cyril had been a sergeant in the RAF, serving in Egypt and India during the war, more quarter-master than fighting man. He too was an easy-going person and could be very entertaining at parties, his *pièce de résistance* the sand dance, performed with a fez which always had my auntie Rene in stitches. He worked as a counter clerk in the Post Office and was always very careful about his appearance. The couple lived in a maisonette in Casewick Road, half way between Norwood High Street and Leigham Court Road which led to

Streatham. In the evenings he liked to frequent the bar of the nearby Norwood Lawn Tennis Club, of which in my teens I was a member. The couple had two sons, Trevor and Ronald. In age Trevor fitted between Colin and Howard with Ronald the youngest cousin apart from the only girl, the baby of the cousinhood, Geraldine, Vera's daughter. Trevor was always a source of conflict amongst us, somehow managing to annoy everybody except Nanny, who was his sole defender. I always thought it significant that Trevor was the only one that Blackie, as amiable a tail-wagger as one could encounter, took a bite out of Trevor, no doubt responding to some sly act of persecution. But Nanny's sense that there was something amiss in his family life which affected him, proved justified. Relations between Doris and Cyril were plainly deteriorating. Cyril was not in any sense a violent man, neither was he a drunk, though he liked his evening tipple. But he was mean and he kept Doris on too tight a financial rein which humiliatingly obliged her to borrow money from Reg and even on occasions from my mother, who had precious little to spare. I remember bitterly resenting my mother on the occasion she raided my savings bank to lend to her tearful sister, knowing full well that it was never likely to be replaced. Such domestic pressure led to the break-up of Doris and Cyril's marriage and in a somewhat messy fashion. To ease her money worries, Doris took a part-time secretarial job in a plumber's merchant business in the Camberwell Road. The proprietor, Bill Harris, was himself going through a difficult time domestically with a terminally-ill wife and an adolescent daughter, Jo. The relationship between Doris and Bill Harris developed to a point where Doris fled from home, taking Ronald but leaving Trevor in the care of his father. For a time she sought refuge with us. My mother could hardly refuse but from the outset it was clear that my father strongly disapproved and saw things from Cyril's rather than Doris' viewpoint. The atmosphere in the house was fraught and my brother and I were inclined to resent the intrusion and to take the cue from my father. Doris later expressed disappointment that we had not shown greater friendliness to Ronald. The issues eventually resolved themselves. Bill's wife died and Doris and Ron were able to move into his flat in Streatham. Doris duly obtained a divorce and the couple married. These events put pressure on Bill's daughter, Jo, who as soon as she reached adult age left for Australia. The marriage proved happy. Bill was affable and good company. I remember introducing my fiancée to the family at a party in the Streatham flat at Christmas 1962. Unfortunately, there are always victims of marriage break-ups and in this case Trevor and Jo were most affected. Ron, however, benefitted. After leaving school he became an apprentice gas-fitter, good preparation for joining Bill in the business, eventually becoming manager when Bill retired. After Bill's death, Doris inherited the business which, in an age of DIY supermarkets had ceased to be of any great value. However, the large car park behind the shop proved to be a valuable asset. My mother's formerly impoverished sister was now rich far beyond expectation – truly a Cinderella story. Doris lived to be nearly 100, outliving the rest of the long-lived members of the Barker family of that generation and when she died her sons inherited her fortune. Ron had proved to be shrewder and more capable than could have been envisaged. And what of Trevor, the black sheep of the Barker cousinhood? As a young adult he developed surprising flair. Leaving school at sixteen he did a number of jobs including projectionist at a cinema in Stockwell before working in the office of a newspaper. He married Eileen who worked for the Liberal party and soon Trevor popped up as press officer of the Norwood branch of the party, regularly bombarding the local press with propaganda and developing ambitions to become a borough councillor and perhaps even a Parliamentary candidate. The couple lived on Beulah Hill with their two daughters. Unfortunately, this phase of his life ended abruptly in divorce, with alcohol probably among the causes of marital breakdown. His second marriage was opportune – to a barrister with a house in Epsom where Trevor took a job as steward of a local sports and social club. He was by far the most family-minded of the cousinhood and made frequent attempts to bring us together, without it must be said, evoking much enthusiasm. The last time I met him was when I responded to an invitation to an evening at his Epsom club. The legacy from his mother enabled him to spread his wings. He had developed a love of boating and he was now able to sail not merely in local but in exotic waters. Our last contact took the form of an invitation to his Pall Mall club. His legacy, it seems, had transformed him into a man about town. The meeting never happened and in 2018 Ron informed me that Trevor had died suddenly. Ron himself still had a house in south Norwood but had also acquired a villa in Spain. The only cousins to have had a secondary modern school education had outdone the rest of us. That Camberwell car park turned out to be a golden egg.

Doris was not the only one of my mother's sisters to have gone through the trauma of a divorce. Vera, the younger sister, was only in her early twenties when war broke out but she had already married. Both she and her young husband volunteered for the forces, Vera joining the Women's Royal Navy Service (WRENS). During her time in the service she met and fell in love with Cyril Lester, a ship's petty office and paymaster, known to us for several years as 'uncle Pay' until told to call him Cyril. Cyril Lester was also married and father to a son but the affair led to a dual divorce at the end of the war, which must have been traumatic for all concerned. While the tangle was being sorted out, Vera and Cyril lived at '41'. My grandparents must have been shocked by these events, though they were by no means uncommon after the turbulence in so many lives caused by the war but, as always, '41' was a refuge. Vera was a particular favourite of Nanny's whom in many ways she resembled. Slim, lively, delighting in company, she had an indefinable touch of glamour which marked her out and had clearly besotted Cyril. The son of a Wolverhampton manufacturer, public-school educated and so obviously middle-class, to be thrown on the mercy of a working-class family in such circumstances must have been humiliating for him but he coped well. He was urbane, had impeccable manners and a good sense of humour. He would never quite gel with his new in-laws but Vera's charm eased relationships and they were very plainly a devoted couple. As Cyril rehabilitated his career, becoming first an assistant bank manager then a manager, they drifted out of the family mainstream, living first over the bank in Dulwich, before moving out to Beckenham and then Hayes. I remember visiting the Dulwich flat accepting an offer of help from Cyril with my maths, never my strong suit. It was good of him to give me his time because, in order to get together the money needed to buy their own house, he was moonlighting as a croupier in a London casino. The couple had one daughter, our youngest and only female cousin on this side of the family, whom they sent to a private school in Dulwich. I got on quite well with Geraldine but she had all the makings of a 'Sloane' and in terms of career she never seemed to do anything of interest. Hanging around the Dulwich tennis club without actually performing on the courts and taking part in amateur dramatics seemed to be the limit of her interests. Unsurprisingly she was generally perceived in the family as being spoiled with her father the main culprit. As they moved away, we saw less and less of the Lesters. Geraldine married and had two children, but divorced and did not marry again. Vera got on badly with her father-in-law, who perhaps had never quite got over the marital antecedents. I met him a couple of times and got on well with him, receptive to his stories about dealings in aircraft parts with the Air Ministry during the war. He invited me to visit him in Bournemouth where he lived in retirement with Cyril's sister. There I met John, a slightly autistic young man who, I conjectured, might have been Cyril's son by his first marriage. When Cyril retired he and Vera moved several times, including to the Algarve and the Isle of Wight, before settling in Storrington in Sussex. Geraldine lived nearby with her two children, her ex-husband reportedly 'on the skids' in Los Angeles where he had been working for an airline. Vera and Cyril attended my wedding in 1963 and my mother's funeral in 1995 but shortly afterwards Cyril too died. Before long Geraldine reported that Vera was suffering from dementia and eventually had to be moved to a care home where, very highly strung, she had a difficult time. Geraldine's appeals for family visits were largely in vain because of the distance involved. Not long after Vera's death she phoned to tell me that she had been diagnosed with incurable lung cancer. I regret that, knowing her theatrical tendencies, I only half-believed her. It turned out to be the truth and Geraldine died while only in her early sixties. I have since had no contact with her children, though I believe they were both embarked on successful careers.

Brothers

If time and tide eroded the links between cousins, brotherly love is conventionally imagined to be more permanent, though the examples of Cain and Abel, Romulus and Remus and any number of others serve as a warning that it is not necessarily so. My brother Ian and I were very close as small boys, literally so as we shared a bed. I remember our ebullient efforts to kick one another out of it. To be braced against the wall was the strategic position, our energetic efforts curtailed only by shouted threats from below, never implemented. I have hazy memories of a nightmare stay in a children's hospital where we were both sent to have our tonsils removed, as was the brutal custom of the day. I repeatedly tried to get out of my cot to climb in with my brother, only to be roughly strapped down. Nanny gave me a small silver money box shaped like a pillar box which took sixpences until full when the top would fly off. It went into hospital with me but it didn't come out. By the time we had finished our war wanderings we returned home to separate bedrooms – he naturally had the larger of the two from which I was relentlessly repelled. Attending school, we were in different classes and formed different friendships, though some semblance of brotherly love is indicated by a story I fear I have often repeated to my family. I astonished the headmaster one day by successfully spelling 'Renaissance' on the blackboard. 'Go home, Roger', growled Mr. Brennan, 'I can't teach you anything.' 'Thank you, sir' said I, 'can I take my brother?' And together we skipped joyously off into Norwood Park. This may have been the high-water mark of our relationship, as the almost two-and-a-half-year difference in our ages began to have its effect. Not only did we form separate friendship groups but our interests diverged markedly. Ian was always more practical than me. He enjoyed working with his hands, making and tinkering. Throughout his life he would tackle projects for which he had no training – striping down a car engine, installing central heating, etc. – in the firm belief that if someone else could do it, so could he. In my eyes his self-confidence reflected obstinacy bordering on arrogance. It's hard to live with people who never admit to error! He was also materialistic and as an adolescent would get involved in dubious activities which caused my parents some concern. He would help my father with his DIY and gardening, not out of filial duty but because he enjoyed doing it. He was popular with other members of the family for his willingness to help out. These characteristics put him on the same wavelength as my father, creating a genuine cultural gap between the pair of them and me. By contrast, although not entirely incompetent with screwdriver, drill or paintbrush, I took no pleasure in such activities. They were a diversion from what I preferred doing, the dichotomy between hand and head. I preferred reading, spending time in the Upper Norwood public library, which Howard Barker always said was the seedbed of his intellectual journey, and filling notebooks with the beginnings of a story which somehow never got finished. I was no swot. I was passionately into ball games – football and cricket, at both of which I would represent the school and would continue to play into my twenties, and later tennis and table tennis from the age of ten or eleven. Ian had no time for such pastimes but did enjoy cycling and swimming. In this, respect, too, our paths diverged and in truth never really came together as we each pursued our own purposes. In Ian's case this ultimately meant conforming to my father's hopes for our futures, not out of filial obedience but because they coincided with his own. Ian was bright enough to pass the 11-plus exam and was offered a place at Archbishop Tenison's Grammar School, one of the smaller London grammar schools and, for us, inconveniently placed at a distance of at least six miles from Norwood. He was placed in the C stream, an antediluvian practice of internal division which still persists in some schools, as if the selection process at aged eleven was not enough. He never rose above the C stream and never really tried to. His school reports, initially complimentary, increasingly told of a lack of interest and commitment. He didn't like the school and the school didn't much like him. The only teacher with whom he had any rapport was Mr. Conacher, the woodwork master. At fifteen he left to take up an apprenticeship in the print trade as a mounter, making the blocks that held the type. My father was delighted but it was my mother who had to confront the headmaster since the school expected pupils to stay on at least to complete GCE. The gulf between us widened. He was now a wage-earner, enjoying his new-found spending power and sharing my father's Woodbines. He had a reputation for open-handedness but little of his largesse was ever directed to me. At eighteen, his apprenticeship was interrupted by National Service, in his case serving with the RAF in Iraq and Jordan. By that time he had a steady girlfriend who religiously made a weekly visit to our house and even came on holidays with us, her expectations of marriage made very clear.

Ian, guarding the airfield

When Ian returned to 'civvy street' it was almost my time to enlist, which I did in September 1955, also in the RAF and also as a radar operator. His girlfriend, Ann, was the youngest of the four children of Mr. and Mrs. Ball, who owned a strategically placed newsagents and a sweet shop on the corner of Westow Hill and Westow Street, Upper Norwood's High Street.

Her steadfast hopes were realised. They were married in the summer of 1957, Ian aged 22 and Ann 20. To my surprise Ian was insistent that I should be his best man, evidence of residual fraternal feelings that I suspect he had but so rarely showed. At the time I had been given leave to return from my unit in Germany to play in the RAF Championships at Wimbledon. Being best man on the Saturday, their wedding taking place at Christ Church with the reception at the Queen's Hotel, led to my being scratched from the singles, so I fulfilled my fraternal duty knowing that I would have a few awkward moments on my return to my unit with my CO, a fanatical sportsman who had always facilitated my tennis. I covered my dereliction by pleading an ankle injury.

Ian and Ann began their married life, in a manner not unusual at that time, by moving into the Ball's home in Orleans Road, a street of middle-class houses in the valley between Central Hill and Beulah Hill, with a recreation ground known as the 'rec' situated between the two. Ian came under pressure from his father-in-law Dick Ball to join him in the business and he agreed to do so. My father was made very unhappy by this decision, partly because it meant abandoning a trade for which Ian had served a five-year apprenticeship but also because Ann's elder brother, Cliff, was already working in the business. The fear was that, should anything happen to Mr. Ball, Cliff was would inherit and Ian be reduced to the status of a mere shop assistant or be forced out. Ball's newsagents was a well-established local family business. It cannot have been easy for Ian to make the switch. Both father and son were large, taciturn men with a disconcerting disdain for small talk. It came as a surprise to learn that in his younger days Dick had played double-bass in Ambrose's well-known orchestra and retained a keen interest in popular classical music and that Cliff was following in his footsteps as a player of the double-bass. As it happened things turned out well. Cliff left to establish his own shop somewhere in Essex and Ian increasingly took control of the business. Mr. Ball kept to his word and Ian and Ann inherited the shops on her father's death. He injected the business with new energy, establishing a flower shop adjacent to the newsagents.

He was soon able to buy a house at Orpington, where his four children were born and, with business flourishing, they moved to a larger house and garden in Beckenham. The 70s and 80s were the days of his pomp. He acquired a Jaguar, presided over garden parties at Beckenham and began to cut a figure in the Norwood Chamber of Commerce. Of the four children, the eldest, Tony passed the 11-plus and attended St. Olave's, a well-rated London grammar school that conveniently migrated from its ancient site in the City of London to Orpington. Christine and Linda attended local schools while the youngest, Raymond was sent to the prestigious fee-paying school Alleyn's in Dulwich. Full credit to my brother for his energy and appetite for work but his over-optimism, so much in contrast to the outlook of our father, proved to be his downfall. My warnings about the changing nature of the High Street – with the arrival in Upper Norwood of two supermarkets including a Tesco plus Asian-owned 'all-nighters' – were waved aside as the musings of an academic with no experience in the real world. With the growth of car ownership too, commuter patterns were shifting. Not for much longer the regular footfall, to-and-fro from the bus-stop outside the shop; the morning paper and on return *The Evening News* or *Standard* and perhaps cigs and sweets. First to go was the flower shop and then, most especially distressing to Ann, the Beckenham house. Ian and Ann were reduced to living above the newsagents in a flat which he himself impressively created with the help of a part-time assistant, the remarkable Eric who had been shot in the spine when intervening in a robbery, but remained bravely agile. Hubris. Finally, Ian managed to salvage enough from the sale of the shop to retire to a one-bedroom bungalow in Hythe in Kent, a popular retirement spot for South Londoners, Norwood by the sea. He died of lung cancer, aged 79 in 2014, to be followed three years later by Ann. In spite of his abilities and his appetite for work, over-confidence and a certain arrogance had brought him down. Although our relationship in adulthood was cordial and never reached breaking-point, our worlds were far apart and I can think of no instance in which my advice or my opinions, even perhaps my very existence, had ever had more than a marginal effect on the way he lived his life. Fortunately, for she lived alone for many years, Ian was devoted to our mother and would regularly spend his lunch-hour with her. He used his practical skills to rebuild and modernise her kitchen, though characteristically he sent her away while the work was in progress and did not consult her about the fittings. To the end, he knew best. A strong character whose self-belief in his latter years betrayed him. Why didn't he ever realise that it was me who knew best!

A Typical Family Saga?

At the risk of claiming too great a pretention, setting this brief family chronicle in the social history of the period does prompt some reflections which may be of general relevance. First education. As far as I can ascertain none of my parents' generation, the Ward six and the Barker five, were educated beyond the age of fourteen and yet among them there was a high level of literacy and articulacy. This was no doubt down to their natural abilities but it also reflects credit on their schools. Modern pedagogy has transformed the school experience and the old practices of rote learning reinforced by the teacher's stick stand condemned. Yet it does seem to have achieved much in a short time. Even my father, the least literate of the cohort, had neat, modelled handwriting, clearly the result of standardised classroom drill. The social mobility that several family members achieved no doubt owes much to enhanced opportunities over time but also sheds a favourable light on the educational grounding which was the work of the Victorian and Edwardian education system. A strong work ethic was a feature of that generation. The shadow of the depressions of the early 1920s and the early 1930s was an incentive to seek and maintain steady employment, as was the very limited outside assistance available before and even after the establishment of the welfare state in 1945. It seems not illegitimate to trace the weakening of the work ethic to the increasing availability of state assistance in more recent years. What stands out in the cases of both Ward and Barker families is the reduction in family size. In the case of the Wards two of my father's brothers had no children and only my father had more than one. In the case of the Barkers none had more than two. Was this a reaction against perceived hardship inseparable from the experience of large working-class families or was it down to the more widespread existence and acceptance of contraception? Probably a mixture of both. Finally, divorce: the incidence of divorce in the older generation of the Ward family was nil. In the Barker family, two of my mother's sisters divorced, though one in the peculiar circumstances of wartime. In the next generation, however, there was a marked increase, five of my cousins going through the process of divorce. A less stable or perhaps a less static society, in which old taboos were eroding?

'Hood and Home'

Ours was a small world in which most relationships were confined to a couple of streets, let alone the neighbourhood. The Bloomhall estate was socially homogeneous in both family and occupational terms. There was a small minority of households containing an only child but the majority consisted of families with two or more children. The great majority of mothers did not work and, if they did so, it was on a part-time basis. The fathers were mostly blue-collar workers, generally in manual occupations, though a few were clerical, employed in lesser administrative roles and fewer still were self-employed. Relationships within the 'hood' were surprisingly formal. The old adage that 'good fences make good neighbours' might have been a bye-law for the estate. Except for the children there was very little in the way of visiting others' homes and neighbours generally addressed each other in formal terms – Mr. This and Mrs. That. Social interaction was largely on a family basis and communal activity, such as the VE day street party, was rare. Only in the case of family tragedies were there manifestations of communal identity: when my father died in 1965 my mother received a cardboard sheet signed by all the neighbours in the street expressing their condolences. Within the collective category 'blue-collar worker', there was of course considerable variety of occupation as exemplified by our immediate neighbours in Durning Road.

Semi-detached, the Ward family shared a pathway and a gate with the Bates family. Mrs. Bates could have been a figure out of Coronation Street or East Enders. A bottle-blonde who, unlike my mother, was quite prepared to be seen in a headscarf and slippers and frequently had a cigarette dangling from her lips. Her favourite brand was Craven A, I know because I was ofttimes despatched 'down the alley' to the nearest shops to renew her supply, though the promised sixpence did not always materialise. She was in the habit of borrowing small quantities of tea or sugar, repayment, as in the case of the sixpences, rarely made. But she was a cheerful, inoffensive lady and one could imagine a far worse neighbour. Her husband, Jack Bates, was a fireman who went through life silently except for the steady thump-thump through the party wall of his double-bass, his hobby and part-time occupation being to play in a jazz band. He was kindly and I particularly remember – with some embarrassment – an occasion on which I came home from school desperate for the toilet, only to find the house empty and locked. I cacked my pants and howled with distress. Jack Bates heard me, filled a bucket with warm water, came round and cleaned me up. Very neighbourly and not forgotten. Both their two sons were older than Ian, the elder Teddy having served in the navy. Cheerful and happy-go-lucky like his mother, he tried various jobs before ending up as a butcher in a horse-meat shop in Brixton market. The younger, Phil, was street-smart and 'a bit of a lad'. Taking up the bass like his father, he did so successfully, his band at one stage performing at Ronnie Scott's, which was establishing itself as the nation's premier jazz venue.

The Bates were a great contrast to our neighbours to the right, separated by pathways and a fence. The Wilsons made it a point of principle to 'keep themselves to themselves'. The husband was a furniture removal man, gloomy and unapproachable. If a ball went over the garden fence, a not infrequent occurrence, we were always doubtful of its likely return and if by him, it would be with bad grace. Mrs. Wilson was less daunting, a brisk, efficient woman with a strong Welsh accent but, like her husband, very private and not on Christian name terms with any of her neighbours. Their two sons, Jeffrey and Ivor, were a little younger than us and never allowed to play out in the street. I never on any occasion crossed their threshold: how the boys' birthdays were celebrated I never knew and neither were they invited to our usual gatherings with games, jelly, sandwiches and the exchange of small presents. The Wilson's semi-detached neighbours were the most interesting family in the street, the surname suggestive. Mrs. Gent, a kindly, homely and much put-upon little woman known to us as Kate (a most unusual familiarity) was the only single mother that I was aware of on the estate. Her household was peopled by four children: the eldest, Joe, had mental health problems and was rarely seen outside the house. Two more sons, Alan and Geoff, were both older than Ian and finally a daughter, Daphne, a strong, handsome girl who needed to be and was very resilient. Alan and Geoff were very boisterous and often quarrelled violently. I remember seeing them wrestling at an open bedroom window, each trying to push the other out, which, if either had succeeded might have had fatal consequences. Not a little of what had affected Joe, is seems, ran through the family. They didn't play in the street with us younger children but I never found them unfriendly and was not a little intrigued by them for it was evident that they were a-typical and not only because of the constitution of their household. On occasion admitted into the house I was surprised to find that among their possessions were such treasures as butterflies mounted in a mahogany box and stamp collections. The sense that the Gent boys were somehow different was reinforced when both were admitted to the elite Dulwich College. Given their circumstances it seems unlikely that this was on a fee-paying basis, so it was assumed that they had won scholarships. But on reflection perhaps not, because rumours suggested that Kate had been housekeeper in a wealthy household and that all four children had been sired by her employer. The name 'Gent' acquired new significance. Was it a pseudonym? I never found the answer. As far as I am aware, the boys held their own at Dulwich College but going to such a 'posh' school marked them out and sometimes dangerously so. I remember seeing Alan and Geoff surrounded by a taunting ring of local boys on the fringe of Norwood Park on their route home from school. Fortunately, they knew how to handle themselves and needed to. In later years I learned that Alan had become a PE teacher but, as to Geoff, I knew nothing of his fate, nor that of Daphne and their mother Kate.

Living opposite was the Kidd family. The eldest of their four children worked with his father, a self-employed builder, then came two more sons,

Tony and Barry, who were close in age to Ian and myself, Tony becoming Ian's closest friend. Their 'afterthought' was a girl, Eileen, who much to our amusement couldn't pronounce her Ks, calling herself Tidd. Most of my friends lived in the 'Pan', a circular cul-de-sac with at its centre a planted area surrounded by a low railing. It was an ideal play area, safe from local traffic which was anyway sparse. In the ring of houses lived families from which playmates emerged and, on most days, the 'Pan' hummed with life – various chasing and hiding games, miniature cricket with wickets drawn in chalk on a convenient wall. Where did those lumps of chalk come from which also marked out every suitable pavement for the purposes of hopscotch? Among the 'Pan's' families I can recall were:

The Murphys: father a fireman. One daughter, not allowed out to play.

The Peareths: father a decorator employed by the council as was their eldest son. Two further sons, one Ian's age and a daughter. Massive CPFC fans, trooping off on Saturdays enveloped in Palace scarves.

The Leeks: father self-employed in nobody knew what. Owned small pre-war Fiat, one of only two cars in the street. Two daughters, Jean and Iris, smart and comely. Keen Girl Guides but not great joiners in street games.

The Harrises: two children, one of whom, Kath, was our baby-sitter on the rare occasion that our parents went visiting. Very studious girl, responsible and tweedy as was her elder brother. Concerning her father, more anon…

The Hollises: father in the removals business. Owned the other car which I don't ever remember seeing on the move. No tax? No spare parts? Three children, the eldest Mary handicapped but mobile and with a formidable clout when responding to insults. A second daughter, Audrey, was a happy, sunny girl, the street favourite. For a time Audrey and I were inseparable, she quite happy to join in football (usually in goal – after all she was a girl!) and cricket. She was nearer in age to Ian who eventually replaced me in her affections. Was it something I didn't do? Then there was a younger brother, Freddie, a scruffy laid-back lad who turned out to be good at maths and eventually followed me to Archbishop Tenison's. We played a lot of chess together and after Freddie the pieces needed a good wipe. Hygiene was not a strong point in the Hollis household but it was the most free-and-easy house in the street, perhaps because Mrs. Hollis had a full-time job.

The Fowles: father a white-collar worker, perhaps a clerk, employed by Lambeth Council. Three children, the eldest Jeanette was my brother's first girlfriend, pretty and demure. Two boys, the elder Richard, a very easy-going and good-natured lad, my closest friend in the street.

The Norfolks: three children, the eldest a girl called Rae, then two boys Johnny and Jimmy, the latter with a crippled leg requiring a special boot. Johnny had a gravelly voice which could always be heard above the fray. More about Mr. and Mrs. Norfolk anon.

Politeness to adults, a degree of privacy and mutual respect, above all upholding one's reputation in the neighbourhood – respectability – these were the communal values in our social stratum. Those who offended against these mores were inevitably singled out for whispered gossip, often literally over the garden fence and picked up by young ears. There were a number of offenders. Take the case of Mr. Harris, the admirable Kath's father. During the war he had served as a commissioned officer in the Marines but post-war failed to find a job that he felt to be commensurate with his status and abilities. He was a stiff, unsmiling man and the fact that he was seen to be about in the day time exposed him as being unemployed in a street where every male held down a job. He was nicknamed 'Mr. Never-Works' and cold-shouldered by neighbours. Mr. Norfolk worked as a mechanic in Norwood bus garage and always looked as if he had just crawled out from under a bus. A silent, solitary man, he was nevertheless the indispensable source of the ball-bearing wheels which were an essential component of our homemade trolleys, the others being planks from some bomb site and orange boxes from the grocers. He was widely regarded as a possible cuckold. He was not the object of gossip, it was his wife. She worked full-time and on many evenings she would set off for a rendezvous with an unnamed and possibly apocryphal paramour at a local pub. We would hear her clattering up the road from her house on the corner of the 'Pan' in her high heels, dyed black hair piled above a painted face. Her behaviour earned her the nickname 'Dirt & Diamonds'. The third most egregious offender against the local sense of respectability and the worst was Mr. Burgess, a stocky coalman whose red face revealed an over-indulgence in booze. He earned a reputation as a wife-beater. Mrs. Burgess was a kind and gentle soul who most certainly did not deserve what was visibly meted out to her. The Burgesses had two children, a boy my age and a girl, the former given the nickname Buggy as a result of the discoveries of a school nitty nurse. Poor Mrs. Burgess would plead with me and others not to call him Buggy but he himself never seemed at all fazed by it and to this day I can't recall his actual name.

It is to the credit of my mother that she never – unlike the Wilsons – attempted to confine us to home and garden. She insisted on good behaviour and trusted that we would not get in to mischief, at least not into anything serious. She sometimes required a little help in the home, an errand or two and on Mondays, help with the mangling in the days when the week's washing required a series of stages: boiling in the copper, scrubbing on the washboard (an implement later pressed into service for musical purposes by the skiffle groups of the late 1950s and 1960s), rinsing in the sink before being passed through the thick wooden rollers of the mangle and then being hung out on the washing line in the garden. Mondays during the school holidays were a dismal scene. Mother with her hair in a scarf and a determined look on her face, the kitchen filled with steam and condensation and the floor scheduled for scrubbing once the operation was complete. All hands to the washing line should there be rain once the washing was out. And finally, a cold meal on Monday evenings, the remains of Sunday's joint served with fried potato and pickle. The advent of a washing machine, a top-loaded variety equipped with rubberised wheels for mangling, was a godsend to my mother, as for housewives everywhere, greatly reducing the drudgery of Monday washday. Those heavy old mangles could then be disposed of to the rag and bone man, a regular visitor to the area with his horse and cart and his unintelligible cry to announce his presence. For years after the war, too, the dairies in our area used horses. A particular favourite was an Express Dairy milkman called Tom Sargent and his docile horse 'Strawberry", which knew the round as well as Tom did so he had no need to brake the cart or lead the horse, as he moved slowly from house to house, thus saving Tom time and effort. Other milkmen were not so lucky and it was not unusual to see a horse mount the pavement to nibble the privet hedges. Some local milkmen would employ a boy. The more generous would pay 2/6d, the stingiest 1/6d. Boys – never girls as I recall – would wait outside the dairies where the carts were loaded to offer their services, in the case of the Express Dairy, this was in Westow Street near to Mr. Ball's newsagents.

If not required for home duties or otherwise employed, we were free to roam. This often meant simply playing in the street or in the local park handily situated at the end of Durning Road. Norwood Park was a much-valued amenity. Not only did it provide ample space for spontaneous games of football – coats down for goals – and cricket but there was also a well-designed and equipped playground with a slide and a variety of swings and roundabouts, some of which would have horrified modern advocates of health and safety. There was also a sand-pit for young children and a pavilion to sit in and provide shelter in the case of rain, all supervised by a lady in her own little hut, from which in my experience, she rarely emerged. The playground was surrounded by railings which were not a serious obstacle after closing times, the only hazard being the brown-suited park attendants who patrolled the park, in which case a speedy exit over the railings was called for. The park was our Wembley, our Lord's, a space to play and meet with friends.

The street and the park were our playground but, of course, many hours were spent indoors. My mother was a reader and I soon acquired the habit. She did not, however qualified, offer me guidance in the choice of reading and I was largely unaware of the existence of a body of children's literature. I would browse the fiction shelves in the Upper Norwood Public Library picking out the names of authors I may vaguely have heard of. I remember reading at an early age and possibly with little understanding, works like Charles Dickens' *Bleak House* and Sir Walter Scott's *Ivanhoe*. But my favourites were Westerns and these I borrowed not from the library but from our travelling librarian who visited regularly with his van packed with books; newer books 6d, older ones 5d or 4d. My mother, largely out of sympathy, usually borrowed one or two and the librarian, whose name I never knew, would ask 'would Rog like a book?' And when Rog did it was invariably a Western by authors with names like Zane Grey. Clearly an educated man, with a 'posh' voice, our travelling librarian may have been the victim of the Depression of the 1930s, when it was not unusual for such men to become self-employed in this way. A family friend, Mr. Teague who lived nearby was an example. A civil servant who lost his job, he took to selling tea around the area until later able to find employment again. His wife worked part time in a grocer's shop in West Norwood and some years later when in my teens was instrumental in getting me a job as their delivery boy, hauling a bike front-loaded with boxes up and down the area's hilly streets on two evenings a week and Saturday mornings. On the lighter side there were popular comics, the *Beano*, the *Dandy*, the *Wizard*, and the *Hotspur*, which most children enjoyed and would be regularly swapped among friends. In the Beano, the world's longest-running cartoon strip, Dennis the Menace and Minnie the Minx preached anarchy to its receptive young readers. 'Break the Rules', but we seldom dared. Later more sophisticated comics such as the *Eagle* also appeared. Strip cartoons would invariably figure German soldiers in various stages of defeat, uttering such phrases as *Gott in Himmel*. Some much-envied families had relatives in less straitened places such as the USA and Canada and would receive parcels which would include comics as well as food and clothing. One of my closest junior school friends was Peter Dixon, whose family lived in a spacious flat in an Edwardian house in nearby Whitely Road. The Dixons had relatives in Canada and Peter's home seemed to me to be a veritable treasure trove. His mother, an ex-nurse, worked as a dinner lady in our school and his father was a white-collar worker. They would sit down and play cards with us, their favourite game being solo whist. Peter's father, Frank, would on occasion join us for cricket in the park. Any boy such as Peter, who owned a cricket bat and ball and a football, did not lack for friends.

Before the 1950s, the few homes equipped with television sets were the envy of their neighbours, and especially their juvenile neighbours who were all too prone to peering through their windows for a glimpse of this new phenomenon. In the 1950s the number of owners of sets increased steadily and it had become common by 1955 when ITV was launched to complement and to rival the BBC. When I left home in that year to join the RAF, the Ward household still had no set. The up side of this was that the quality of my homework may have benefitted from the absence of this distraction. The vast majority of families, however, were equipped with radio, with thirteen million licences in circulation. In those years of austerity in which we huddled round fires fuelled by an utterly inadequate coal ration in the cold, dark winter evenings, the radio was our window on the world and our main source of entertainment. *The Third Programme* was for the intelligentsia, high-minded talks and discussions and classical music, not geared to the likes of Durning Road. Then came the *Home Service* but it was the *Light Programme* which featured the most popular shows. A gallant band of comedians and comediennes laboured to keep up the nation's spirits and none more so than Tommy Handley, the comedy voice of the nation, much as Vera Lynn was the nation's songster, though the almost-forgotten Ann Shelton was also very popular. Being a comedian in the 40s

Tommy Handley and the cast of ITMA

and 50s was no easy occupation. The tight, censorious grip of the Reithian BBC ruled out anything remotely scatological or thought to be in bad taste. Even the *double entendre*, the stock-in-trade of British comedians, suffered from the censors' blue pencil – even something as innocuous as 'winter draws on' was likely to incur disapproval. The comedians were obliged to fall back on sketches and funny characters in a way that would seem utterly unsophisticated to an audience today. Handley's *ITMA (It's That Man Again)* featured characters such as the office cleaner Mrs. Mopp and the tipsy Colonel Chinstrap who furnished the nation with catchphrases – how, I wonder, did Mrs. Mopp's opening address to Handley, 'Can I do you now, sir?' escape the censors? To this day I find myself repeating one of the stock sayings of another ITMA character, Mona Lott, 'it's being so cheerful as keeps me going'. When Handley died suddenly in 1949 the nation, about half of which tuned into his weekly Thursday evening programme, mourned and he well-merited the tribute of a memorial service in St. Paul's cathedral.

Among other cheeky chappies in the Handley mould were Arthur Askey, capitalising for all he was worth on his diminutive stature, and Ted Ray, star of the long-running programme *Ray's a Laugh*. In the course of the 50s and 60s comedy tended to become more sophisticated, with programmes such as *Round the Horne*. Kenneth Horne and Richard (Dickie) Murdoch often employed now forgotten wartime references such as Horne's frequent (and always interrupted) 'When I was in Sidi Barani...', this being our only notable military victory in 1940 over the Italians in those desperate years 1939-1942. Another justifiably popular show was *Take it From Here*, featuring Jimmy Edwards' not entirely untrue to life irascible, cane-wielding headmaster. Much of the improved quality of the comedy of this period was down to the writers themselves and to notable performers such as Frank Muir and Denis Norden. Comedy shows were complemented by variety programmes, which would usually include a ventriloquist as well as comedians and singers, quiz shows including the very popular 'meet the people' formula of Wilfred Pickles' *Have a Go* and prototype 'soaps' such as *Mrs. Dale's Diary*. Other favourites included detective mysteries solved by the suave Paul Temple and the breathless nightly derring-do of Dick Barton and his intrepid companions Jock and Snowy. During the day programmes such as *Workers' Playtime* and *Music While You Work* were broadcast from factories, all serving to cheer up the nation in those drab and dispiriting post-war years. If homework was an unloved chore in many of my evenings, my mother, while listening to the radio, darned. Unlike today's cotton-rich socks, holes seemed to appear daily and required regular darning. I remember having to learn this skill myself while doing National Service: after an initial allocation all additional clothing had to be paid for and included in the initial hand-out was a 'hussif' (housewife) containing needles, thread and darning wool. Over two years one learned to be quite proficient. Most housewives also knitted and my mother was no exception. She usually had a cardigan or jumper on the go. Knit one, purl one, drop one…spare hands would be required to help transform the skeins of wool into balls. Mum couldn't afford to buy all the wool needed for a garment in one go, but she obtained her materials from a small kiosk in Chapel Road run by a charming lady with a crippled leg who would put the wool aside until required and was also a fund of helpful advice. It would be many years before I actually purchased a cardigan or a pullover, until that time mine would either be hand-knitted or hand-me-downs, as were other items of clothing – one of the disadvantages of having an elder brother.

Domestic entertainment was relatively sedate and for greater excitement it had to be the cinema, which enjoyed a great wave of post-war popularity. Many people attended more than once a week and evening queues were invariably long. With names such as 'Regal' and 'Rialto', with lavish decors of plaster gilt and murals in the foyers, the cinema chains offered a contrast to the drab and dilapidated state of much of urban Britain and complemented the glamour of Hollywood productions such as *Gone with the Wind*. Prices were reasonable and within the reach of most families; the coveted back row was 2/4d, the middle tier 1/9d and the front rows 1/3d, with the cheapest child's seat 9d. Films rated 'A' were barred to children unaccompanied by an adult but in practice it was not difficult to find a familiar or a friendly face in the queue to take one in. The usual fare was a main film, a 'B' film (very often a Western), a newsreel from

Pathé or Movietone stridently delivered and perhaps a cartoon thrown in as a filler. When one programme finished the next followed promptly and it was possible to hunker down for a re-run if so inclined. When the final programme finished the national anthem was played and those who hadn't left early to avoid it stood quietly. Usherettes with flickering torches were employed to help people find empty seats in the crowded rows, their other role being to sell ice-creams either during intervals or by making themselves available at the rear. British film studios such as Ealing contributed some excellent films but couldn't match Hollywood for glamour and, as in popular music, it was American productions which offered the contrast to their own dull lives which people sought. Upper Norwood boasted two cinemas very close to each other in Church Road and there was a larger one in West Norwood which featured a Saturday morning session, price 6d for children. It was pretty basic fare – cartoons, an otherwise uncommercial film, often a Western, a serial which was always cut short at a moment of extreme peril for its heroes and heroines to ensure subsequent attendance, all accompanied by a non-stop deafening noise from the juvenile audience. Attendance soon palled and I gravitated to mainstream as soon as I could.

Cinemas were, of course, a haven for courting couples, the back row being especially coveted. To invite a girlfriend to the cinema was very often the opening gambit in any relationship. Being seen with a girlfriend in the cinema was sure to be reported to one's mother. In my case she might enquire who I had been seen with and did so in a manner which often seemed accusatory, reflecting her obsession with 'respectability'. The query would usually evoke a denial. I was in my twenties before I brought a girlfriend home. The cinema apart, there were group visits to swimming baths at Forest Hill and Thornton Heath and in summer to the Brockwell Park Lido and for a time roller-skating at a rink in Brixton was popular on Friday evenings. Funds were always short and constrained what we could do and how often we could do it, making the radio in particular the principal source of entertainment. Many people were surprised to learn from Harold Macmillan in 1957 that they 'had never had it so good'. Such rose-tinted politician-speak was, to say the least, premature. In that year I was still darning socks as I saw out the remains of my National Service in a billet in Germany.

Better-off families could manage a week's summer holiday, usually spent in resorts on the Kent and Sussex coast. We managed a few, Margate, Broadstairs and Southsea among those I recall. But I regret that they were far from the highlight of my year. I empathise entirely with George V, who when dying in 1936, refused to consider convalescing at the seaside, his last words reportedly being 'Bugger Bognor'. The typical seaside boarding house would be in a large forbidding Victorian or Edwardian terrace offering B&B and an evening meal ('kip and kipper'). They were typically presided over by someone the satirists personified as 'Mrs. McGurgle', who might have been trained in the Third Reich. Landladies had to wrestle with the same problems of supply as every housewife so that the fish and chip lunch in a newspaper were far more appetising than standard boarding house cuisine. Rules were restrictive, reinforced by parents anxious not to offend fellow inmates: hush-hush in the bedroom, keep voices down in the dining room, leave buckets and spades in the porch. Beaches, especially sandy beaches, held no charms for me. I lacked any urge to build sandcastles and preferred swimming off a shingle beach. If the weather was indifferent the days could drag: highlights would be spending one's saved-up pennies in the end of pier slot machines and giggling at Donald McGill's inevitable postcard display. His brilliant array of grotesques – fat domineering ladies, skinny hen-pecked males, vicars and scout-masters. McGill's attempts to make the nation laugh earned him time in 'clink', sentenced for obscenity, which says volumes about the repressive attitudes of the day, especially towards all things sexual. McGill, master of the double or even triple entendre, incidentally, was buried near my family plot in Streatham cemetery on his death in Balham in 1962.

Bandstands and brass brands were still happily in fashion and sometimes talent competitions were staged, in one of which I remember taking part but inexplicably my genius went unrecognised. At home father would occasionally parade his talent as a tap dancer but he refused to enter, using as his excuse that there was no sideboard to hang onto. Plentiful ice-creams provided some solace but not nearly as much as the sight of the train pulling into the station to take us back to East Croydon and on to Gipsy Hill. Fortunately a cheeky and cheerful entrepreneur was on hand, striving to transform the typical working class holiday into something gayer. This, of course, was Billy Butlin, who in the 1940s was expanding his Holiday Camp empire, mainly in the north of England. My father was perspicacious enough to add Butlins to his modest portfolio, but never treated us to the experience. Lest I appear too curmudgeonly, I did enjoy day trips to Brighton and on one occasion a few of us from the 'Hood' cycled the 52 miles, had a swim and cycled back totally exhausted. Mrs. McGurgle and her like was ultimately undermined first by Billy Butlin then the Spanish costas.

While Butlin was busy transforming the British holiday experience, another entrepreneur was attempting the more fundamental task of transforming the British shopping experience. From humble beginnings selling surplus NAAFI stores in Hackney market, Jack Cohen was building the retail behemoth which became Tescos. I think of him as the inventor of the supermarket trolley. Supermarkets based on the principal of self-service were late on the scene in Norwood. Throughout my boyhood, as a loyal Labour-supporting family, we shopped at the Co-op at the bottom of Gipsy Hill in the traditional way. Mum made a weekly list in a well-thumbed little book and put in the order which was delivered not by horse like Co-op milk but via an electric van. If shopping in person, the items would be gathered by an assistant and piled on the counter for transfer to the customer's bag, no baskets, no trolleys. Grains and pulses were weighed from the sack, which not only cut down on packaging, but also created a warm pervasive aroma in the store. The cash would be screwed into a container and zipped by a wire to a cashier in the gallery, the change returned in the same manner. If possible non-grocery items were also bought from the Co-op which every year declared a welcome dividend, 'the divi'. I also saved up my shillings in the Co-op Savings Bank, my balance rarely exceeding two pounds. Fresh vegetables and fruit were bought on Saturday mornings at Lawrences in Westow Street, a busy open shop where piled stalls protruded onto the pavement. In spite of rationing, queues were ubiquitous, something else that Jack Cohen, knighted in 1969, sought to reform. Tescos was another share that my canny father ('always follow the housewife') added to his portfolio.

'School days are the happiest days....'

I remember my primary school years as stable and contented. Of course as
children we were aware of the many shortages and discomforts imposed
by the country's state of impoverishment and the governments' austerity
measures but, unlike the adults, we did not share memories of better
days. I had the benefit of a secure home background, parents who bravely
battled the problems of the day, friends, family and the freedom to roam.
Expecting less, we learned that in a time of austerity material things did
not come easy, that if you couldn't make it yourself (scooters, trollies, basic
toys, etc.) you had to save for it and if possible earn the necessary funds
by running errands, doing paper and other delivery rounds, helping the
milkman and so on. Visits of uncles and family friends were made all the
sweeter by the half-crown customarily handed over at parting. My first
bike cost £3 and it was acquired as a result of small sums accumulated
in my Co-op Savings Bank account. It was by no means the real deal, not
something the champion cyclist of the day, Reg Harris, would have given a
second glance but it could be upgraded by investing future savings. Much
the same applied to sports gear, cricket bats, footballs and later to tennis
equipment and items of clothing. Such things didn't come easy but they
materialised and were perhaps better appreciated for the effort put in. I
had enjoyed my Cleethorpes primary school and I look back fondly on my
three years at St. Joseph's Catholic primary school, part of the sprawling
Catholic establishment which stretched along one side of Central Hill and
Crown Dale, an easy ten-minute trot from our home, making it possible
to return home for lunch. Although it cannot be said to have done a great

deal for my father, he always spoke well of it, giving it credit at least for trying. The school lay behind the continuous wall built of London brick, which protected the Catholic establishment from the outside world. It was an unpretentious single-storey building constituting a line of classrooms flanked by a glass-covered corridor on the other side of which were cloakrooms and the offices of the headmaster and his secretary. There was a small playground for infants and a larger one for juniors bounded by another wall beyond which were the Convent woods, a tantalising area which forever remained a mystery since the wall was too high either to climb or to see over. The toilets were separate from the main building, the urinals unroofed. All in all, a simple but homely building.

My memories relate mainly to the top two classes and their teachers. The first was presided over by Miss Garland who left a considerable impression. In her early thirties I would guess and to me glamorous. She had dark, wavy hair and a healthy complexion and wore clothes which clearly did not come from our local Co-op. She spoke very precisely and correctly, maintained strict discipline but also displayed a softer side. I still remember with embarrassment an occasion in which I stood beside her desk gripped by an affectionate arm, going through an essay in which, to her

amusement, I had spelled the word 'suit' as 'soot'. I felt very much that I was one of her star pupils and another was a boy who was obviously in dress and speech more middle-class called Anthony Leggett. We became friends and for a time I was a frequent visitor to his home in Eversley Road, on the 'posh' side of the 'Rec' and close to Beulah Hill. His father

Skinny kids. PE class at St Joseph's 1940s

was, I believe, a civil servant and both parents were plainly well-educated. He had a younger brother, who introduced me to chess and then ran rings around me though he failed to put me off the game. Also a sister, Claire, with a long dark plait that I always longed to pull but with difficulty refrained. She was the first girl who ever appealed to me as more than a potential goalie and in her company I felt a little tug at my heart strings. The Leggetts did nothing so rough as kicking balls around on the 'Rec' even though it was outside their front door but they had a variety of hobbies. One of Anthony's was classifying trees and collecting leaves which would then be pressed into notebooks. Miss Garland lived with her parents in a Regency house on Sydenham Hill, the ridge above Dulwich near to where Joseph Paxton must have lived, which was a paradise for tree-huggers. She invited us to visit, which we did. Claire would beg to come with us on our expeditions only to be brutally rejected by her brother, upsetting her and causing me silent anguish. It was a friendship which couldn't last, he a loner with highbrow tastes and me more gregarious and more proletarian. One might say that football came between us. But I am grateful to the Leggetts who gave me a glimpse of a different lifestyle, as indeed did Miss Garland. Another friend I remember for very different reasons was a handsome younger boy of Italian origin called Alphonse Abasela, who took a real shine to me and constantly sought my company. He was a really nice kid but he had one very off-putting feature, he smelled heavily of garlic, then unknown to the British cuisine and which I found offensive. Large intakes of water which he endured did little to remedy the problem, cutting short a beautiful friendship.

My most long-standing friendships were both with boys called Peter – Peter Dixon and Peter Hurd. Peter Dixon worked with me at one time to produce a newspaper, *The Norwood Imp*. He shared my urge to cover every blank sheet of paper with scribble but to bring thoughts to a coherent conclusion was a skill largely denied to us. We also organised a football team whose principal opponents were the boys of Christchurch choir, much envied because they were paid for singing at weddings and other occasions. But, as described earlier, Peter had the great advantage of being the recipient of parcels from Canadian relations and at every opportunity I spent time at his house in nearby Whitely Road. For both his parents it was a second marriage, his mother was a Catholic and brought Peter up in that religion while his father was an Anglican and had a daughter, Sheila, by his previous marriage and both attended Christchurch on Gipsy Hill. Peter's sister, a wispy blonde, was engaged to one of the Gandy twins, from a family who lived on our estate but of the rare white-collar variety. Her fiancé, tweed-suited, learning to manipulate a pipe and correct in all things, was a perennial butt for Peter and myself and would retaliate by the stock response of the twenty-somethings – 'wait till they get you in the army'. Both Peter and I ended up in the RAF and both as radar operators.

The other Peter, Peter Hurd, was a perennially cheerful and ebullient boy, keen on football and never without a ball to kick against kerbs and walls and my companion when we first ventured to Selhurst Park to watch Crystal Palace FC, then perpetual stalwarts of the Third Division South. We would argue furiously about the respective merits of our favourite footballers. I was loyal to Ted Broughton, the player who kindly took my autograph book into the dressing room making me reluctant to admit that his nickname 'Granny' had more than a little justification, while Peter's idol was a tricky little winger called Clough (no, not that Clough). Peter lived in a flat in nearby Alexandra Drive with his parents and baby sister Lesley. His mother was asthmatic and I remember with horror seeing her almost choking as she tried to tell me where I could find Peter. His father managed the fish shop in West Norwood High Street, part of the MacFisheries chain, and was the rare owner of a car, I think a Morris with the temperature gauge on the front of the bonnet. On several occasions I joined the family on day trips to the coast, a rare treat. Peter and I would irritate his father by disputing the respective merits of the AA and the RAC as if they were Broughton and Clough. Most cars in those days sported one of their respective badges and would be acknowledged by their roadside patrols with a salute as they passed by. The Hurds owned a bungalow in Orpington which had been occupied during the war by a refugee family and they had some trouble getting it back. When they did they moved there and, although I stayed with them a few times, we inevitably drifted apart and I lost a best friend and a fellow CPFC supporter.

The top class at St. Joseph's was massively dominated by the headmaster, Mr. Brennan, who regularly tested our spelling and times tables with rod in hand which, though it could be brought down on a desk with a terrifying crack, in my experience was never used on juvenile flesh. Mr. Brennan was a figure of respect bordering on fear. He was a tall, rangy, dark-haired man with sallow cheeks and red-veined face who spoke with a strong Irish accent. He seemed to have access to a secret source of information, perhaps from on high. On Monday morning he would castigate individuals for not attending Sunday mass or attending but at a later rather than an earlier service. A perennial victim was a boy called Willie Robinson, son of a council painter and decorator from our estate. I often wonder what happened to the hapless Willie, was he scarred for life or was the verbal lashing the making of him? The school was very strong on numeracy and literacy and I can't imagine that any child left the school illiterate or innumerate, though otherwise the curriculum was sparse and left few memorable activities or excursions. As a relatively bright member of the class I was never the recipient of a tongue-lashing and Mr. Brennan, in spite of appearing often to be the agent of the Vatican, or at least the local priest, never seemed to discriminate against his non-Catholic pupils. There was one advantage to being in the non-Catholic minority. The local priest, Father Larkin (inevitably known as Father Larkin-About), a fat Friar Tuck lookalike with a bulbous nose, visited regularly, usually near lunch-time, to test the children's knowledge of the Creed and other doctrinal elements. As a Protestant I was exempt and would slip off for an early lunch. However, I did not entirely escape the *odium theologicum*. For a time I felt great awe for the Roman Catholic religion and would call in to the church on my way home from school and sit for a few moments contemplating the iconography. If there were nuns in the church, so mysterious and ethereal, so much the better. For a long time I felt that Catholic notions of sin, confession and forgiveness made perfect sense. I imagined the soul as a white box and sin as black spots which could be erased by confession.

By the time I left St. Joseph's my fear of Mr. Brennan had evaporated as I increasingly detected the twinkle in his eye and that a kind heart beat beneath the formidable exterior. This was confirmed later when I re-visited the school and was always greeted warmly. Looking back, I realise that Mr. Brennan had a decisive influence on my life, making a decision which was well-intentioned but perhaps not for the best. In 1946 my brother passed the 11-plus exam and left to join Archbishop Tenison's Grammar School. I was in the class below and at the age of nine clearly met all of Mr. Brennan's expectations in terms of literacy and numeracy. When the time came to administer the 11-plus exam there may have been an absentee or absentees and Mr. Brennan included me in the group taking the exam. I passed and this posed the question of whether I should follow my brother into the grammar school. I have vague recollections of Mr. Brennan suggesting that I might stay on and apply to a boarding school such as Christ's Hospital and my mother insisting that I should follow my brother to ATGS. This I duly did, arriving on the first day of term in September 1947 a week before my tenth birthday and more than a year below the average

ATGS 1st XI 1954-5. Author front row, extreme left

age of my class. I must have been considered up to standard academically as I was promoted after the first year's exams from the 'C' stream to the 'A' stream, but in other respects – physically and perhaps emotionally – I was probably ahead of myself and under stress. Secondary school life in 1947 was in so many respects tougher and more exerting than it would become a generation later. There was also, as I shall recount, later complications posed by the next tier of examinations, the GCE 'O' level with an age expectation of sixteen. Inevitably I reached that starting line too soon and would be what in the RAF would have been called 'back-flighted'. Mr. Brennan had, quite unconsciously and with the best of intentions, complicated my educational odyssey.

Just as attending a denominational school had the effect of separating my brother and I from neighbouring children, so going to different secondary schools separated us from schoolfriends. No other boys from St. Joseph's went with us to ATGS. Some, including Peter Dixon, went on to a Catholic grammar school, Clapham College, and others to Salesian College. A number of my old schoolfriends joined a youth club run by a Catholic church in West Norwood. I joined them on a number of occasions but for the first time felt that I no longer belonged: different schools and perhaps even different religious allegiances, though I felt none beyond attending a school with a strong Anglican identity, took their toll and proved to be alienating. My friendship with Peter became sporadic and being on opposing sides in a football match between our two schools (ATGS won!) was one of the last occasions on which we would meet. After National Service he worked for Shell, married a girl we had been at St. Joseph's with and settled in the district while I sought pastures new.

The basis on which I was allocated to Archbishop Tenison's Grammar School remain a mystery to me. The only *raison d'être* I can discern being that I was following in the footsteps of my brother. Having an elder brother in the school was not in my case an asset. It was soon apparent that the heavily academic curriculum was suited neither to his tastes nor his talents and he served unfortunately as an example of the inflexibility of a tripartite system which appeared to have no mechanism for transferring individual children to a more appropriate form of education, which in his case might have meant transfer to the Brixton School of Building. Ian spent as many hours as he could in the workshop, a small building in an angle of the playground separate from the main school. On reflection, Ian's alienation was not unjustified. Non-academic subjects were relegated to minority time with little more than a genuflection towards Art, Music and the crafts. Fortunately, Ward junior adapted better to the prevailing ethos, though my performance in the main science subjects was never more than laboured and to drop them in my fifth year came as a welcome liberation.

Tenison's, with a school roll of about 450, was one of the smaller London grammar schools, the size of its intake limited by the cramped nature of its site in Kennington Oval. I knew nothing of its history and the school did nothing to enlighten its new pupils. How much more appropriate would it have been to learn something of its origins and to foster pride in their new school in first year history instead of being confronted with the arid study of Babylon and Ur. Its story contained much of interest. The school had been founded in 1685 in the crypt of St. Martin-in-the Fields by its vicar, Thomas Tenison, Charles II's appointee. Tenison later repaid the Merry Monarch's patronage by responding to what purported to be his dying wish ('let not poor Nelly starve') by preaching a sermon at the funeral of his favourite mistress, Nell Gwyn, in 1687. Later, having been consecrated Archbishop of Canterbury, Tenison crowned two monarchs, Queen Anne and the Hanoverian George I, before his own death in 1715. Meanwhile, the school that came to bear his name was transferred to the site of a former hotel in Leicester Square in 1695, ultimately moving in 1928 to a purpose-built neo-Georgian building in Kennington where it remains. Thomas Tenison's contribution to education included another Archbishop Tenison's school in Croydon and a girls' school, St. Martin-in-the-Fields, which came to rest in Upper Tulse Hill. He also counts as a pioneer of co-education, all in all, a notable contribution to society and reason to be proud of the Archbishop's crest which adorned our blue blazers (the sixth form wore black) and his coat of arms on the metal badge which adorned our caps (sixth form exempt). Something of the school's history could be garnered over the years from Founder's Day ceremonies held in St. Martin's and from Speech Days, which on occasion figured descendants of the founder such as Colonel Tenison, Alderman of the City of London. However, I wager that many boys left Tenison's knowing nothing of its history. Equally there was no formal introduction to the four worthies who had been selected as names for the houses into which the school was divided – Arnold, Hogarth, Hunter and Newton – mainly for the purpose of sports competitions. What identified one's membership of a particular house was the colour of the peak on the school cap, in my case brown for Hogarth (named, of course, after William Hogarth, the great eighteenth century artist and satirist) of which I later became captain. The colour brown was the dullest of the four, but at least it coincided with the colour of the caps worn by our Surrey cricketing heroes ('the Brownhatters'). Of the four worthies Arnold (Thomas, not Malcolm nor Matthew) seems the most appropriate. There was little in the regime at Tenison's that the famous nineteenth century headmaster of Rugby School would not have found familiar.

It was with a mixture of expectation and trepidation that I set off to my new school in early September 1947, a few days before my tenth birthday. Anyone living more than five miles from their school was provided with a free travel pass stipulating the route and the times of travel. Our route began at the bus stop on Central Hill where we boarded the Number 2 bus, which took us through West Norwood, Tulse Hill, Herne Hill and Brixton to Stockwell, where we disembarked and sprinted down the escalators of the underground station to board the Northern Line to travel the one stop to Kennington Oval, after which a walk of a few hundred yards took us past the great ornamental gates of the famous Oval cricket ground to our red brick building on the opposite side of Harleyford Road. Psychologically the association with Surrey CCC was always important to those of us passionate about cricket, which included my mother, who often accompanied me to Test matches at the Oval and sometimes Lords, beginning with the Aussie tour of 1948. In most of the years of my time at Tenison's, Surrey, blessed with a host of stars, headed by the Bedser twins, and the 'spin twins' Laker and Locke, Peter May and others, was the dominant team in the county championship. By some mysterious process of osmosis, in spite of the front windows in the upper floors being out of bounds, the whole school seemed to be aware of the state of play at any given time and there was perturbation when, on what in those days were rare occasions, Surrey's imperious dominance was threatened. In the days of uncovered wickets Laker and Locke held sway. Relations between the schools and Surrey CCC were excellent, the school was allowed two games annually on the hallowed turf and invitations for boys to come and spectate were sometimes extended. Coming back to Kennington on a Saturday was no chore if it was to see a Test match rather than serve a detention.

On first acquaintance the school was not prepossessing, a contrast to the homely junior school from which I came. The building had suffered considerable damage during the war and repairs were still underway. The top storey which had housed the gym had been destroyed and needed re-building and, while this was ongoing, the Oval Long Room had been made available. I was able to boast, apocryphally, that I had leap-frogged over the bust of W.G. Grace. The playground, already too small, was littered with builders' materials and overcrowding led to clashes and fights. Boys would form a ring around the combatants and urge them to 'fight, fight, fight', which they did until staff arrived to break it up and lead away the combatants for punishment. Welcome to the Blackboard Jungle. Corporal punishment was endemic and routine from the headmaster down. There were exceptions who never or rarely had recourse to the cane, though the penalty for their forbearance might be greater difficulty in class control since the degree of respect accorded was related to their disciplinary reputations. For most of us, Saturday morning detention loomed larger than three of the best as punishment. Few of that generation went through school uncaned, including myself.

All Teachers Great and Small

The accent on strong punitive discipline came from the top, from the headmaster Dr. P.H. Robinson MC MBE and to a lesser extent from his deputy Mr. Butler, whose main deterrent was less the cane than his role in deciding who should be condemned to detention. Both men were comparatively elderly, Dr. Robinson having served and been wounded in the first world war. He was short, no more than 5'2" or 3" and stooped, the rumour being that he had a steel plate inserted in his shoulder, accounting for the nickname 'Hooky'. Such disability, however, did little to slow him down. He seemed always to move at high speed, unexpectedly popping up in corridor and classroom, catching pupils in a range of misdemeanours and doling out appropriate retribution, from rebuke to the cane. He had a short fuse and would sometimes interrupt morning assembly, leaping up from his seat to complain angrily about the desultory rendering of the morning hymn. As I recall the only hymn sung with any gusto was the one beginning 'Lord dismiss us with thy blessing' at the end of the term. As befits an Anglican school, there was also a prayer and a bible-reading, after which he would order 'send in the Jews' and a column of boys would enter to hear the day's notices and, if appropriate, sports results. The bible reading was done by prefects and I was once deeply embarrassed by a practical joke played on me when it was my week. Before leaving school I would check the reading and put a bookmark in the bible ready for the next morning. Someone never-identified shifted the bookmark and I found myself reading a passage of the Old Testament which listed a long line of 'begats'. After a minute or so, I was sternly interrupted, no doubt red-faced, and ordered to find a more appropriate passage. Great jape but one that more than strained my sense of humour. Dr. Robinson was hardly a *simpatico* figure, irascible and distinctly short on humour. As a physicist himself, he favoured the sciences over the arts and was also the enthusiastic commanding officer of the cadet corps (RAF) and disapproved of the minority who resisted joining, which included me. So I was a little short of brownie-points on both counts. But there was no doubting his commitment to the good management and to the welfare of the school. In my final year I enjoyed a more personal relationship with him as I recognised that he was giving thought to the most appropriate course to take for my future. Like Queen Elizabeth and Raleigh's fart he had quite forgot the bible-reading incident and my recalcitrance over the corps and in return I quite forgot the occasion when he caned me for being sent off (unjustly, of course) by the referee who just happened to be a master of the opposing school in a first XI football match. Quits.

Dr. Robinson's deputy 'Joe' Butler was of the same generation and also a physicist. He was bald and wrinkly, his appearance tending to validate Darwin's *Origin of Species*. When listening to schoolboy excuses, every conceivable version of which he had heard a thousand times before, he would pretend deafness, stoop over his victim with cupped ear and repeat 'whatssat Johnny?' In his role as guardian of the Saturday morning detention list, the only strategy likely to win a reprieve was to claim selection for a school team. Mr. Butler never taught me; hardly a matter of regret, though if he had done so perhaps I would have seen a different side of him. I suspect that he had a sense of humour which found little outlet in the punitive role of chief hanger and flogger, the role traditionally accorded to deputy heads.

With only one exception, the masters who taught me science (or attempted to) remain a blur in my memory. The on-going shortage of teachers of the science subjects and maths tends to validate the notion that the general quality of teachers in those areas was less than in the arts. My own predilections, of course, were also a factor in my underwhelming performance. The one exception to the forgotten parade was Mr. Hibberd, a rangy, cadaverous man with an over-large nose, always dressed as if he had just survived a nuclear explosion. In chemistry lessons he seemed to spend most of his time deep in his cupboard, from which he would emerge from time to time to quell the rising tide of noise. On one occasion, he made the mistake of adding to his rebuke the phrase 'under my very nose' and a quiet voice was heard to respond 'we can hardly help it, sir'. Incidents such as this can enlighten the dullest of lessons and this is, I fear, the only reason that I recall Mr. Hibberd.

The teachers who taught the subjects from which I did derive satisfaction remain clearer in my memory. My first form master, who taught Latin and who was also responsible for the under-14 football eleven for which I played for two years, the second year as captain, was Mr. Hopwood. He was a short, stocky man, always dressed in brown tweed which gave him the appearance of a small brown bear. He was kindly and never in my recollection resorted to the cane. Its common usage by other masters made maintaining discipline more problematic for teachers such as Mr. Hopwood and in retrospect I feel that he could have been more forceful. Reprimanding those who neglected their Latin grammar homework or showed insufficient leadership on the football field did not come easily to him. Guilty on both counts.

Insufficiently forceful was hardly a criticism one could ever have levelled at Mr. Waddington. The most handsome and patently the fittest member of staff, a veritable ball of muscular energy, he was in charge of PE and the top storey of the building where the new gym was situated was his domain. He was a keen rugby player, his club the London Irish, and also an amateur boxer. His efforts to introduce rugby to the school fortunately failed but he did manage to train a few boys to enter the London schools' boxing competitions. The new gym was state-of-the-art and Mr. Waddington would drive us up the brand-new wall bars and ropes and over a variety of box horses. Ex-navy, he had a voice that could have been heard in a force five gale off Scapa Flow. He had a habit of yelling 'Geronimo!' at a distance of about six inches from the face of 'slackers' who showed an absence of the kamikaze spirit, amongst whom I must confess I would include myself. Mr.

Waddington had a permanent influence on me, instilling in me a lifelong hatred of gymnasiums. I was simply too small for the size of the obstacles he confronted me with and for him I had only one use. Since I was small but quick on my feet he would send me into the ring against boys he was training for competition with instructions to keep moving and ducking. The instructions were entirely superfluous. He also enjoyed British bulldog. What's a little bloodshed among fellow scholars? On occasions when the sports ground at Motspur Park was unusable, Mr. Waddington would preside over a class debate on some topical issue. I would be cast in the role of chief defender of the Labour government and soon find myself in a minority and under attack from that element of the class which travelled down the southern region from such posh places in leafy Surrey as Raynes Park. As I remember, I had only one stout ally, a boy called 'Inky' Hammond, an avowed communist who lived in a prefab in Kennington Park. By the time we had reached mid-school, 'Inky' was looking distinctly middle-aged, very mature for his years and with nicotine-stained fingers. He was clearly talented and contributed a humorous column to the school magazine under the pseudonym Clarence Blott. At some point and to my regret he seemed to disappear, leaving me to imagine him composing anarchist pamphlets in a dingy back-street office off the Charing Cross Road. There were precious few lefties at Tenison's and no-one, not even me, was quite so left as 'Inky' Hammond.

Much as I admired Mr. Waddington as a specimen of manhood and for the power of his tonsils, his interest in sports in no way coincided with mine. In my second year I was selected to play for the under-14 football team and I particularly remember the joyous occasion since I scored twice in a 5-2 victory, a scoring feat, alas, that I don't recall ever repeating in my passage up the school and into the 1st XI. I remember telling my mother about my triumphant debut and, true to form, she commented 'I don't suppose you were any better than the other boys'. No doubt true but somewhat deflationary, as it was intended to be. Tenison's as a footballing school struggled to hold its own against the grammar schools which constituted our perennial opponents. Not only were several larger but some had playing fields attached which made practice possible. I always wonder why greater recourse was not had to nearby Kennington Park, but the school sports ground was situated at Motspur Park, several stops away on the southern region. On sports afternoons we would trek the few hundred yards to Vauxhall station with its long gloomy approach tunnel, board the train and then at the other end be faced with another walk to the sports ground. On match days, Saturday mornings, one found oneself often playing with fellow team members with whom there had been no chance to practise, hardly a recipe for cohesive team work. That the first XI of which I was a part managed to give a reasonable account of itself was largely down to two outstanding players, our captain Fred Hall and a boy called Weller. Playing in a school team would take up most of my Saturdays during the soccer season. Going to the meeting point at Vauxhall if we were at home, playing and then wearily returning home by train and bus. On one occasion the Old Tenisonians, who used the ground on Saturday afternoons, arrived two players short and I volunteered to stay on to make up the number. I arrived home truly knackered and took a couple of days to recover. It was the one and only time that I played for the Old Tenisonians as I failed to join that organisation when I left school, largely I suppose because of the hiatus created by National Service. I didn't play football for another team until I turned out for the Old Grammarians, the Old Boys' Association of Battersea Grammar School some years later.

Equally keen on cricket, I managed to get myself selected for the under-14 XI and to make my mark as a batsman. Alas, success can come too soon. In the following season I was selected for the school second XI and I found myself out of my depth, playing with older and bigger boys. After suffering a succession of low scores my confidence took a dip and I decided that giving up Saturdays in the cricket season, only to spend the preponderance of that time either fielding or sitting in the pavilion, was not the most felicitous use of my time. I made myself unavailable for selection and although attempts were made later to lure me back by those who recalled that I had once been a promising batsman by dangling before me the chance of selection for the school's two Oval matches, I held out and never turned out at cricket for the school again. I always enjoyed the game but my future appearances would be limited to friendly matches for various XIs captained by friends and acquaintances plus school and college matches during my teaching career.

I can't remember whether on my initiative or his, in the holidays Peter Dixon and I began to play tennis on a tarmac court on the nearby 'Rec'. I was soon hooked on the game but Peter dropped off so I joined a small club nearby. I quickly felt I had outgrown this club and searched around for an alternative. I found it in West Norwood, at the bottom of Knight's Hill and close to the bus garage. It was a gem of a club, small with just a few hard courts, one floodlit, a good standard of tennis and with exceptionally good table tennis teams, a pavilion with a bar and a kitchen where a local lady called Eileen would serve up snacks and light meals at weekends and after matches. It also had an active social scene, dances and cabarets organised by a committee which included a couple of members who worked for the BBC. For some five years, between the ages of 13 and 18, West Norwood LTA became the centre of my sporting and much of my social life. The standard of the tennis was not as high as that of table tennis, our teams containing several players of county and national standing, but it was nevertheless solid and competitive. As my game improved so I began to enter tournaments. One organised annually by the *Evening News* was particularly popular: one received a card through the post bearing the name and contact details of one's next opponent and so on until defeated. As one progressed so the numbers were whittled down and I would eventually be drawn against a boy called Terry Densham who became a friend and to whom I always lost. He had great natural ability and became a table tennis international at fourteen and Surrey county junior tennis champion. He also beat me in the final of the South London under 18 table tennis championship. In the summer holidays I entered some junior tournaments, preferring to choose venues in the county of Kent rather than in Surrey, where the standard tended to be higher. After playing in a few tournaments, I was offered free coaching at the hands of a Captain Rogers, who had his own little tennis school in Beckenham. A perennial problem for me was that tennis was expensive, club fees and the cost of equipment far exceeding my pocket money. Needless to say I received no help from my father who took no interest in any of my sporting activities, so the deficit had to be filled by working. A morning paper round brought in 6/6d, a grocery delivery round in West Norwood on two evenings a week on the way home from school and on summer and Saturday mornings, bridged the gap. The downside was that this expenditure of time and effort inevitably took its toll on my academic work, with homework corners cut and especially at the expense of those unloved science subjects. I have no doubt that becoming a reasonably accomplished tennis player then and in later life broadened my horizons, remaining the central feature of my social and leisure life over many years.

Counterbalancing my ignominious performance in science and maths was better progress in English and History and to a lesser extent in French, Latin and Geography in which my achievements were passable. In terms of my relationships with staff my closest connection was with the English staff and principally with one of the only two female members of the school staff Miss Lefa Fry, of whom I have the warmest memories. Miss Fry was, I would judge, in her thirties, short and stocky with strong features and always soberly dressed. She had a poise and a natural dignity that commanded respect and had no difficulty in controlling her classes without recourse to threats, let alone punishments. She managed to convey to us semi-savages that to misbehave or show bad manners was to violate our status as gentlemen. In short, she was a natural and well-respected teacher. I was fortunate that she took an interest in me from my first year and this rapport continued for the length of my time at the school. I remember that on one occasion she sensed that I was backsliding and at the end of a lesson walked me round the playground, ticking me off but in a positive way that demanded a positive response, which she got. Her love of her subject shone through, especially for poetry though I have never understood nor shared her passion for Gerard Manley Hopkins. It was through her that I was awarded the English prize in the lower sixth and through her that I eventually became editor of the school magazine,

The Tenisonian. She also prevailed on me to take part, against my initial inclination, in a number of school plays. Miss Fry lived with her parents in West Norwood, near to where I had been born and on one occasion I was invited to visit, perhaps to borrow a book or books. Our relationship did not end entirely happily. She was very disappointed that I ultimately chose to specialise in History rather than English as I contemplated University entrance and sat scholarship exams in the upper-sixth. My head prevailed over my heart. At the time I was thinking of journalism as a future career and History seemed to me likely to be of more utility. But she, far more than the History staff, left her mark professionally and personally. Her principal colleague in the English department was an intriguingly exotic character, Mr. Laidlaw-Brown. Apparently, he had been a captain in the army during the war but anyone less likely to have waded through muck and bullets it is hard to imagine. He was fastidious and a conscious dandy. Smartly and fashionably dressed he had the courage in those drab days to wear suede shoes and yellow socks and his hair was coiffured and lightly blued. The boys drew what to them was the obvious conclusion; his nicknames were 'Rodney' and 'the Poof'. He sailed through the world utterly unperturbed and smelling faintly of pomade. He spoke very precisely, with a twang of Edinburgh Scots and a habit of exaggeratedly rolling his rs: to hear him analysing 'verbs of incomplete predication' was an education in itself. He seemed to look down on us humble creatures from a great height and had no disciplinary troubles. Unlike Miss Fry, he had no hesitation about caning and his right arm was in no way effeminate. He lived in Chelsea and brought to the staffroom a touch of Boho. He was a character but not one I could easily relate to, at least until I got to know him better, which I did mainly through taking part in the annual school play. He and Miss Fry got on together very well, put a great deal of time and effort into these annual performances and demanded much from the cast. More than I did myself, they saw me as a potential thespian and overcame my reluctance to take part. My first role in my very first year was as one of the fairies (Mustard Seed) in *A Midsummer Night's Dream*. My reluctance was not mainly because I wasn't and never have been an exhibitionist, an essential characteristic of a successful actor, but because of the added burden of the time and effort involved. Rehearsals were held on Monday evenings after school. At four o'clock the cast were given tea, consisting generally of jam or fish paste sandwiches and a rock cake. Readings and then rehearsals followed well into the evening. This inevitably involved much hanging around as one waited for one's scenes. Miss Fry and Mr. Laidlaw-Brown supervised intensely, cajoling us and shaping performance. When released I would set off home, tired and hungry and still facing the unrelenting prospect of three nightly homeworks, which would often be completed on the bus next morning or in the playground shed. Ultimately, of course, we cast members benefitted from the experience. The plays were well received on the three nights they were performed before large parental audiences and there was the valuable incidental benefit of making closer acquaintance with the works of great literary figures. By the time the 'Dream' was performed I knew the play backwards and later participation led me to appreciate the works of Ben Jonson, Richard Sheridan and Bernard Shaw. Because I baulked against playing further female parts as I reached the upper school, the English duo kept me on board by tempting me with the role of *Sir Lucius O' Trigger* in Sheridan's *School for Scandal*. I was meticulously prepared, Miss Fry furnishing me with recordings of Irish poets such as Sean O'Casey to perfect my Irish accent. It proved to be the highlight of my theatrical career and brought me much praise. My mother attended the plays and speech days, my father never on any occasion attended the school. It was in the course of those long evenings and culminating performances that I got to know both Miss Fry and Mr. Laidlaw-Brown in less formal settings. I remember visiting his flat in Chelsea where the cast were measured and fitted by a theatrical costumier. It was through him, too, that I first had the opportunity to visit the Old Vic and to sample serious theatre. I learned to appreciate that part of the art of teaching was the ability to play a role. Laidlaw-Brown was an actor-manqué and a convincing one. He remains, together with Lefa Fry, fresh in my memory after all these years.

The only other female teacher on the staff was Madame Despicht, whose family roots lay in Alsace on the French-German border. Although as conscientious a teacher as any on the staff, she had none of Miss Fry's dignity and composure and she struggled with class control. Her appearance didn't help. She was thin, weedy and slightly stooped with straggly dark hair, resembling nobody so much as the Olive Oyl character in Popeye cartoons. She had an odd lip movement which caused her to spit when pronouncing consonants, leading boys to retreat from the front row or make exaggerated plays with invisible umbrellas. Boys can be cruel and the class of '47 showed her little mercy, at times visibly upsetting her. The most dramatic occasion I can remember was at a time when G.B Shaw's *Arms and the Man* had reached dress-rehearsal stage and I was playing the role of Louka, the scheming maid. I had my costume in a bag with me in the classroom and a couple of the more devilish boys stole a pair of stockings, pulling them over their heads like Chicago bank robbers, while another boy with a classroom key locked the door when the French lesson was due. When Madame Despicht arrived, she was confronted with two stocking-masked faces glaring at her through the window into the corridor. After tugging furiously at the door, which was mysteriously unlocked by the time she returned, she rushed off to the staff room to summon male assistance. In the pogrom that inevitably followed I was able to use my thespian skills to appear a victim rather than a perpetrator and escaped punishment. With the best will in the world Madame Despicht did little to advance my competence in French and left me with a basic weakness in grammar, which the senior French teacher Mr. Lewis ('Lulu') did much to repair at O level and later at A level. He was a firm but friendly teacher who, as we advanced up the school, treated us as young adults and got the appropriate response. His guttural voice – he also taught German - I found somewhat off-putting and he was inclined to favouritism, spending much class time in conversation with Charles Gagliani, whose skills ranged over French, German and Italian and whom Lewis chose to take up a short scholarship to America. But Charles, a friend who lived in nearby Streatham, was the right choice being more suave and mature and better-dressed than the rest of us and certainly the most competent in language skills. I loved the French literature we studied – Jean de la Fontaine, Lamartine, Maupassant, etc. Madame Despicht still has a warm place in my memories for an act of extraordinary kindness. When I was in the lower sixth I planned a trip to France in the summer holidays and a boy called Geoff Scott in the science sixth asked to come with me whilst making it clear that I would be expected to make all the arrangements. It was a curious decision on his part, he knew very little French and we had never been friends. But he was regarded as the brightest kid in the sixth-form and nicknamed 'Brains' or 'Potty Scotty', brains always associated with degrees of madness. Well, two's company, so I agreed. Madame Despicht learned of our intentions and at the end of term presented me with an envelope containing several thousand francs and a list of places I was to visit in Paris, our first destination. To top it off, we were to have a meal at a well-known restaurant in the vicinity of the Champs Elysées, which having hitched all the way from London we duly did. What the haughty French waiters made of two dusty English schoolboys in shorts and sandals and lugging backpacks I have no idea but we enjoyed a meal of, if I remember rightly, *lapin au moutarde*. One doesn't forget such kindness and if Madame Despicht wanted me to feel guilty for past conduct, which I am sure she didn't, she succeeded. A dedicated teacher but, perhaps in the wrong school at the wrong time.

The biggest decision I was to make in the course of my sixth-form studies was to prioritise History over English when considering future university entrance. This was not because of but in spite of the fact that the history teaching and my relations with the two men who taught it was far inferior to my regard for and rapport with my English teachers and especially Miss Fry. The less obtrusive of the two was Mr. Giles ('Farmer', inevitably). He was a tall, moustachioed, correct and impersonal man, the very model of a subaltern who in his regiment might have been in control of stores and noted for making careful lists. This was how he taught history. No anecdotes, no jokes, no personal banter, just carefully prepared notes which passed from his notebook to ours. His lessons ended without discussion and he would leave the library, where lessons for the upper-sixth were held, with an abrupt 'good-day, gentlemen'. I felt the urge to stand to attention and salute, but lacked the nerve. Since Mr. Giles' notes were relevant and well-digested his was a formula for passing exams but hardly the stimulus that one might have hoped for. The other history master, Mr. Birchenough, made an indelible impact from the very first time one encountered him, being a complete contrast to his bloodless and impersonal colleague. Birchenough, wire-haired and with a bristling moustache, had been an officer in the Indian army and in retrospect I think he may have made a considerable contribution to the loss of India. He treated us as if we were sepoys. He regularly stalked the corridors in search of misdemeanours and one could hear him barking commands and reprimands from many yards away. He was well-named because he could never birch enough, carrying out multiple canings on a daily basis. In the classroom he would carry out spot inspections, sending boys with dirty necks or inky fingers to the cloakroom to wash, all the time keeping up a chorus of personal invective through clenched teeth. He would pick on individuals, me not excluded. He would call me Goldilocks and express synthetic sympathy for my parents for having to put up with such as me. I once answered him back and received a stinging punch to the head. He would cane boys who got less than five out of ten in the weekly test, the best incentive for cheating one can imagine. In short, he was a sadist who should never have been allowed near a school or school children. It was a blot on the reputation of Tenison's that he was allowed to behave as he did but it is also a commentary on the times. Most of the masters had spent the war years in the services and witnessed many dreadful scenes, while most of the boys had experienced evacuation, bombing and the absence of fathers – all brutalising influences. This was not the 1960s. Hanging and judicial punishment, flogging, were still current and adult authority in schools and in society went largely unchallenged. My mother's response to my tales of unwarranted punishment was not, I'm sure, untypical: 'I expect you deserved it'. *Autre temps*. Paradoxically Birchenough was a more stimulating teacher than Giles and by the time I had reached the senior forms he had dropped the inquisition approach, although still capable of angry outbursts. Even in junior forms he had used the epidiascope at a time when visual aids or aids of any kind were not widely used in grammar school classrooms. He didn't teach from notes and laced his talks with anecdotes and the odd joke, some of the blue variety. I remember an occasion when he referred to some wretched victim of Charles II's revenge having 'shat himself'. A boy called Connor bravely interrupted him: 'Sir, you have used the wrong past participle'. He survived with his head still in place. Neither of these men dispensed words of praise and encouragement but I was awarded the History prize when in the upper-sixth without comment by either. I asked for Winston Churchill's history of the first world war and was gratified to receive the several volumes. Fortunately, my love of History survived both men. My attitude to Geography was bland, I neither liked nor disliked it, but it did have a value for those of us who disliked science. Under the old matriculation qualifications, a successful candidate had to achieve passes in English, counting as two, Maths, a language and a science and fortunately Geography was accounted a science, so lifting the burden of the 'real' sciences as early as the fourth form. What a relief! Geography was taught mundanely by two men, Mr. Bates and Mr. Hawtin, whom I once managed to astonish by identifying the port of Wei-hai-wei in northern China (information, of course, gleaned from my readings in History). After waffling shamelessly in the 'mock' exam paper in the subject Mr. Bates commented all too accurately, 'never has so much been written about so little'. By threatening to withdraw my name from the list of candidates he forced me to revise in earnest and when the time came to sit the actual exam I performed creditably. I did later, however, find physical geography indispensable in the study of diplomacy and war. And Scotty and I did find map-reading useful in finding our way from Paris, through Luxembourg, to the Dutch coast and eventually to a ferry port and back to Blighty. And, mercifully, it counted as a science.

The Brennan Predicament

Having observed that entering grammar school at a very young age had complicated my existence, when it came to take public examinations it proved something of a nightmare. When GCE examinations came round in the early summer of 1952, I was fourteen. Whether the school made the decision to withhold my candidature or I fell foul of age regulations, I've no idea. But someone somewhere made the decision that that I should wait a year. So, in September 1952 I entered the lower-sixth without O levels to commence study for A levels in History, English and French. This meant putting my seven O level subjects into cold storage until the exam season came round in the early summer of 1953, when I was still not yet sixteen. This time I was allowed to sit the exams, passing in six but failing in Maths which, because of its importance, meant I needed to re-sit at the next available opportunity. In June 1954 I sat and passed my A levels and hoovered up the remaining O level in Maths. Mr. Brennan's legacy had indeed complicated my academic life and imposed a not inconsiderable strain. What to do next? I toyed with leaving school and I recall making enquiries about the Custom and Excise service and the Anglo-Iranian Oil Company, choices for which I now have no explanation. The alternative was to apply for university entrance but, at not quite seventeen, few English universities were likely to be interested and, in any case, the local authority might not offer a grant. However, I was told that Welsh universities were less restrictive. I applied to Aberystwyth University and was accepted by the History department. I now ran up against Dr. Robinson's resistance. He was clearly giving thought to my case and strongly advised me not to take up the place in Wales. I was interviewed by a small committee at County Hall, following which I was refused a grant, whether because of Dr. Robinson's influence or not I don't know. He now advised me to return to school for a third year in the sixth-form during which I should sit selected entrance exams and try for a scholarship. I sat a three-hour exam for Downing College, Cambridge, cooped up in the school secretary's office, as a result of which I was offered a place but with a strong recommendation I should first do National Service. Again Dr. Robinson took a hand. He told me that he had a nephew at Cambridge who had found life very expensive. I suspect that what was uppermost in his mind was the thought that I was unsuitable for Cambridge or, perhaps more kindly, that Cambridge was unsuitable for me. He had some knowledge of my family background, having previously objected to my brother leaving the school prematurely and contrary to its ethos. Perhaps also aware that my father had never attended on any of the school occasions in which I had been prominent. The option he advocated was for me to sit London University scholarship exams and this I did. I vaguely remember sitting with many others in a large, bare examination room, perhaps at Senate House in Bloomsbury, London University's HQ. The upshot was that I was offered a Drapers' Company Arts Scholarship, worth £40 per annum and tenable at Queen Mary College. Better, the scholarship qualified me for the award of a State Scholarship, these being more remunerative than local authority grants, though all subject to means-testing based on parental income. The die was cast and it seemed in a satisfactory way. The Brennan Predicament resolved. My third year, therefore, was largely one of private study for external exams and I often felt rather bored and isolated. Since I was by then a senior prefect and house captain I was fair game for any teacher in need of a dogsbody for some purpose or other. It was, I think, the boredom factor that chiefly led me to decide to defer university entrance and to do National Service.

It was at the end of the autumn term in December 1954 that I enjoyed my first romantic attachment. Up to that time my acquaintanceship with the opposite sex had been limited to mild flirtations with girls on the estate and the near neighbourhood and usually in groups. I met my first steady girlfriend, Julie Bachelor, in a most unlikely setting, the Great Hall of Tenison's school in which no girl had ever previously set foot. The occasion was a joint social between our sixth formers and the equivalent girls of our sister school, St. Martin-in-the-Fields in Tulse Hill. As far as I know this was the first of such occasions. The initiative came not from our sixth form, otherwise I would have been aware of it, nor certainly from our senior staff – neither Dr. Robinson nor Mr. Butler graced the occasion with their presence – but probably from junior staff members, perhaps in an endeavour to soften the macho male culture which was such a feature of those years at Tenison's and probably at comparable London schools. The girls of St. Martin's were being called-in-aid to civilise us and prepare us for the life thereafter, an admirable initiative but inevitably a stilted occasion which, with only soft drinks on offer, took ages to warm up. This was the 1950s, long before the days of rock and roll, bepop and other such fashions. Formal dancing was the order of the day, the waltz, quickstep, fox-trot and tango, with the occasional collective foray in dances such as the Gay Gordons to release the pent-up energies. Few of us had ever had formal dance lessons and we no doubt took a toll of our partners' feet and ankles. The evening began with the boys lined up on one side of the hall and the girls the other, with shy encounters taking place once the recorded music began. I selected a pretty blonde girl and, as was the polite custom, requested the pleasure of a dance. Julie was warm and cheerful company and we spent much of the evening partnered. When the evening ended much more convivially than it had started, the girls trooped off to board their transport home. Julie gave me her telephone number and I promised to call. Our first date followed shortly after in Christmas week. I called for her at her house in Tulse Hill and we took the train from the nearby station to Victoria to see a popular film of the moment, Bing Crosby in *White Christmas*, at the News Theatre. From the time of our first date she had no hesitation in inviting me home to her comfortable family house in Tulse Hill. Her family, father, mother and elder sister, who had been a head girl at St. Martin's, were very welcoming. An *aperçu* into a middle-class home, not entirely strange territory but in all sorts of ways a contrast to the working-class homes I was used to on our estate. Our relationship was easy-going and pleasurable but, alas, inevitably ephemeral. Tulse Hill was not a million miles from home but far enough to preclude casual meetings. Both of us faced exams in 1955 and in my case I was preoccupied with sports and spent much of my leisure time on the football pitch or the tennis court. Tennis was an expensive sport and I needed to work to supplement my meagre pocket money. At that time I was working as a delivery boy for Sidney Ide's grocer's shop, situated almost opposite the West Norwood bus garage and convenient for me to hop off the No. 2 bus on my route home from school on a couple of evenings a week. The job had been obtained for me by a family friend and neighbour, Mrs. Teague, who herself worked there part-time. For my efforts I was paid 10/- a week and it was hard-earned. All my customers lived in streets which stretched upwards from Norwood Road. The carrier on the dilapidated and ill-serviced bike could carry no more than two boxes at a time, any more and it became unstable, and it was impossible to ride uphill. My most distant customer, the Bowthorpe family, lived in a posh house on Beulah Hill and theirs was always the heaviest box of the week. It involved toiling up Knight's Hill before reaching the traffic lights where the Hill met Crown Dale, after which it was possible to ride the half-mile or so along Beulah Hill to the Bowthorpe residence. For my exertions I would be regaled with a sixpence tip. It so happened that the girl in the family was in the same form as Julie at St. Martin's and Julie reported that she was putting it about that she was paying for our cinema visits. Snobbery, jealousy or just teasing? Welcome to the female world. Our pleasant relationship did not so much break-up as peter-out from inconvenience and the lack of available time, but I remember it fondly and hope I learned something about the opposite sex.

1955, then, a year of exams. The decision not to defer National Service arose. This was partly from feeling that I needed a break from study and partly from the popular opinion that, since there was at that time no hint that National Service was likely to be phased out, it was better to get it over with and suffer all the concomitant humiliation at eighteen rather than in the wake of a University education or technical training, when the experience was likely to be more humiliating. To this day I cannot decide whether the decision I made was for better or worse. Was the two years I served in the RAF lost time or was it worthwhile and if so in what respects? What might have been different in my life and career if I had chosen the alternative course? Nearly two million of my contemporaries or at least those who had been faced with a choice must have asked themselves similar questions. In the considerable literature generated by the experience of National Service in the 1940s and 1950s no clear consensus emerges. However, my decision once made, it only remained to arrange with the authorities to be called up promptly following my eighteenth birthday in September 1955 to ensure that I should be demobilised in time to begin the University term in September 1957. The die was cast. My service began on 4 October 1955.

Once the exam cycle was complete I was impatient to leave school. I had no wish to spend the rest of the summer term as a general dogsbody at the beck and call of staff. It was also an opportunity to spend the weeks before call-up earning some much-needed cash. I found a temporary job, ironically in Kennington which meant that my daily commute was almost identical to what it had been for the previous eight years. The job offer was the result of a friendship with one of the top performers at my West Norwood tennis club, Laurie Chapman, who was on the management staff of the headquarters of NAAFI (the Navy, Army and Air-Force Institute) whose ministrations to servicemen I would soon be sampling for myself. The job was a routine clerical one: in the daily post came a bundle of invoices which recorded sales made in innumerable NAAFI canteens scattered around the globe in what was still the crumbling but far-flung British Empire. My section dealt with the navy, including our few remaining aircraft carriers. These accounts had to be checked and filed after which hours of empty tedium remained in which one was expected to give the impression of being meaningfully occupied in order to justify employment of a floor full of staff. I have never been so bored in all my life and those weeks of wasted summer made me determined that I would never in my life take up a desk-bound occupation – better to be a milkman, a postman, or a bus driver like my uncle Reg than to polish a desk chair. It was hard not to feel contempt for those around me for whom this was a way of permanently earning a living and I'm sure that the young 'temps' like myself conveyed this feeling and were resented accordingly. I was also the focus of attention for a group of young female clerks, presumably just as bored, and among the bumpff on my desk would appear the odd note of suggestive enticement. Only mildly flattered, I did not respond but kept my head down. Over this somnolent world my friend Laurie presided magisterially: no wonder he expended so much time and energy on the tennis courts. My call-up came as a relief.

The Call-Up

Of the approximately two and a quarter million young men called up for National Service between 1947 and 1953, more than two thirds were assigned to the army, a very small percentage to the navy and the rest to the RAF, which still retained something of the image earned in 1940-41 in the Battle of Britain, 'the Brylcreem boys'. It was a relief to learn that I had avoided the army and was about to follow my father, my brother and two uncles into the ranks of the RAF. The first hurdle was the medical. All sorts of suggestions circulated at the time of ways to fool the medics, such as by contaminating urine samples or smoking sunflower seeds to simulate lung disease. About 16% of would-be recruits were rejected as unfit, though I doubt that more than a handful of these had ever escaped through such dubious means. Eyebrows were raised as rumours circulated of well-known sportsmen being granted exemption on grounds of having flat feet or dodgy knees. There was also a small number of conscientious objectors and these, unlike in the past, were mostly treated leniently. I passed A1, nothing to boast about, as most recruits did. Following the medical the next stage was to wait for a brown envelope to drop through the letter box containing a postal order for four shillings and a rail warrant; destination Cardington in Bedfordshire, a main reception centre. My father saw me off from the station proffering the advice given by every old sweat to a raw recruit 'never volunteer'. The platform thronged with equally apprehensive lads of similar age with their parents or friends. At the other end, we were bundled into lorries and driven to the base and with lots of shouting and menace herded to our various quarters. The next few days passed in a blur.

One of the commonest threats from the loud-mouthed NCOs, and one of the few not obscene, was that 'your feet won't touch the ground' and they rarely did as we were hustled through a range of procedures. Our locks were brutally shorn by sheep-shearers posing as barbers and, appraised by eye for size, we were loaded up with kit intended to last for the next two years: two uniforms, No.1 for best and No.2 for working, of rough blue fustian; baggy underpants and vests; shoes, socks and PE kit. Shoes and boots without the luxury of fitting and for the first time I was confronted with a shirt with detachable collar and fiddled hopelessly with the collar stud, having been given nanoseconds to get dressed and to line up outside the hut. Personal dignity did not figure on the RAF's priority list. We were soon learning that the screaming dervishes with chevrons on their arms exercised over us the power of life and death. They were vulgar beings the like of which we had never before encountered and devoutly hoped never to encounter again but there were others waiting down the line. A particularly poignant moment was when we were lined up bare-chested

to be inoculated against various viruses. Rumour had it that the same needle was used multiple times until becoming too blunt to penetrate: one or two guys in the queue fainted. There was no time to get to know fellow recruits as we were harried from place to place and I don't recall a single face, even of those I slept next to. What a relief to leave Cardington this old graveyard for dirigibles.

Onward to our next destination for eight

Raw recruit

weeks of basic training. Many rumours about the various training camps circulated ranging from bad to less bad. Those bound for Bridgnorth, I remember, were considered to have drawn the short straw. My fate was to be Hednesford. Fidgeting uncomfortably in our new uniforms and with the rest of our kit stowed in kit-bags marked with our names and numbers, we entrained for the Midlands, further north than I had ever been before. My new persona was AC2 (Aircraftsman second class) Ward. My number – 2772743 – was also engraved on my 'irons' (eating utensils).

Hednesford was one of a number of small mining towns on the edge of Cannock Chase, a fine old royal hunting forest in Staffordshire. The bleakness of the camp contrasted starkly with the beauty of the Chase. As we entered I noticed the whitewashed stones which confirmed the truth of that piece of folklore which stated that everything inanimate had to be painted, the maxim being 'if it moves salute it, if it doesn't move paint it'. Rows of Nissen huts, so named after their designer Colonel Peter Nissen, who would hardly rate inclusion among the nation's most distinguished architects, although he could claim that a large proportion of the nation's youth had passed through his portals, were flanked by buildings essential for the purpose of feeding and training recruits. Also, of course, the parade ground where many hours would be spent as the drill instructors set about the task of turning a disparate group of young men into something resembling a well-oiled formation.

The hut which was to be our home for the next eight weeks was spartan. Rows of beds on either side, each with a locker, the bed space to be immaculately maintained. There was a single stove in the middle of the hut, scarcely capable of heating beyond a few adjacent yards but fortunately, as it was early autumn, its limitations were of no concern. The communal floor space had to be maintained in a pristine state of shine, so having polished and buffed it the inmates then slid up and down on felt pads. Not to travel on a pad would be met with an instant chorus of abuse. The washroom and the toilets (heads) also had to be kept immaculate so that cleaning the premises, never to the satisfaction of our guardians, was a major chore, on top of the hours we were obliged to spend 'bulling' our

Entry to Hednesford Camp

personal kit. Boot polish, dubbin for belts and webbing and metal polish for buttons, all had to be provided by ourselves out of our princely wage of 28 shillings a week minus 3/11d national insurance (this became a particular grievance for me when many years later I found that national service did not qualify as pensionable years).

Our collective experiences did succeed in welding a disparate group of strangers, if not into a band of brothers, at least into a coherent team. The misdemeanours or the failures of any individual were punished as failures of the whole, so it behoved us to work together and do our best to support the weak and the confounded. I still have a group photograph of our flight, 17 in all plus three corporal instructors. Even after the gap of so many years, I am surprised to find that I can recall all their faces though few of their names.

Over the two-month period of pressure the characters of my fellow recruits took shape. The next bed to me was occupied by a gentle and calm older man, married and a father, who had been deferred in order to complete his apprenticeship. He became the helper and protector of the weakest member of the flight, a former public schoolboy called Warwick, an amiable shambles of a lad who found it difficult to co-ordinate any movement and especially marching. He was our 'tick-tock' man, as those

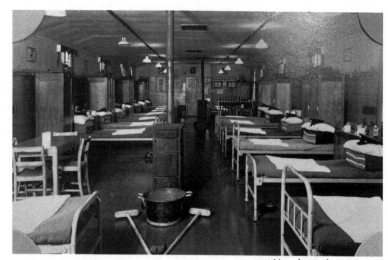

How homely can it get?

afflicted in that way were labelled. He was inevitably the recipient of abuse
from NCOs, much of it a flow of well-practised obscenity. Warwick bore
it all with a martyred air and he certainly needed all the help on offer.
The wonder was that he survived to pass out along with the rest of us,
looking pale and exhausted but managing the shadow of a smile in the
group photo. Another public schoolboy was by far the most professional
of our group, having been an NCO in his school Combined Cadet Force
(CCF) and having experienced many of the drills and procedures we were
put through. An admirable character, he would quietly dispense help
and advice when it was sought and I hope he went on to OCTU, officer
training which seemed to me to be more his natural destination. Officer
training lasted for almost a whole year and was hardly attractive to the
great majority of us. Potential candidates were badgered to sign on for a
minimum of three years and most of those who did so were from public
and grammar schools which had CCFs, which I, of course, had evaded at
Tenison's. Another older man in the flight was chosen to be our senior man
and many orders, reprimands, etc. were relayed through him. Tall and thin
and from Didcot in Oxfordshire, he bore his responsibility cheerfully and
struck up a good rapport with our corporal instructors.

The last roundup. Spot the author

Another older man whose name I do remember because of the impression he made with his gruesome stories of castrating pigs with razor blades, was a farmer from Norfolk, Frank Seppings: the bayonet held no qualms for Frank. It would have been surprising if within the group there had been no clashes. My particular and only *bête noire* was a fellow from Lancashire with a voice that penetrated the hut from one end to the other whose particular party piece before lights-out was a rendition of a popular song, *Cry* by Johnny Ray which struck such a nerve with me that I eventually demanded that he 'come outside'. We were saved by wiser heads from a brawl which could have ended badly for both of us.

Basic training was the one experience common to all National Servicemen and so its routines are fully reflected in the extant body of memoirs and reminiscences. The 'square-bashing', and the endless drills, weapons training, the rifle range, PE, inspections of our persons and our living space, etc. A handful of memories for me stand out. During one of the many early morning inspections an officer proceeded menacingly down the line searching eagle-eyed for poorly bulled kit or a dirty rifle, stopped in front of me and demanded to know whether I had bulled my webbing the night before. Not yet being habituated to the convenient lie, I replied 'no sir'. Taken by surprise, he took a step back and exclaimed 'well, there's one bloody honest man in the regiment' and moved on. For once honesty had proved the best policy. A momentary fear of 'back-flighting' hung over me when I 'failed' a test on the rifle range. This was a perfect demonstration of service logic: my target recorded more holes than the bullets I had fired, apparently thanks to an error by the man shooting next to me. Result, failed.

An altogether nastier incident occurred during a gas exercise. A group of us were ordered to put on masks and enter a small hut and were then instructed to circle around a gas canister. At the command we removed our masks and endured what was probably no more than a few seconds of what I guess was some form of mustard gas. Suddenly the door flew open and we all burst out, coughing and with streaming eyes. Apparently, however, the instructor had not given the order to exit and demanded to know who had forced open the door. Nobody confessed and we were then subjected to a repeat performance. Among incidents which most triggered resentment was to return to the hut after a day's exertions to find bed packs and broken mugs strewn across the floor following an officer's inspection. Bed packs had to be made in a particular way, layered and squared off, while it was hard to keep mugs clean given the nature of the tea, very dark and rumoured to be laced with bromide to subdue the sexual drive. I never found out the truth of that one. A common explanation of the vindictiveness of some officers was that they had failed flight training and resented their new and lesser roles supervising basic training.

The starkness of the camp contrasted with the late autumn beauty of the Chase but our excursions into the forest glades were not altogether idyllic. A night exercise was organised, the objective of which was not altogether clear. But it was clearly expedient to get captured or eliminated as early as possible to spend the rest of the night huddled round a camp fire drinking cocoa, leaving the heroics to the CCF-types. For the remainder of the night we slept under canvas and on the hard ground, trekking wearily back to camp next morning. On the occasional evening we sampled the local pubs in Hednesford or Cannock. The local speciality of 'mixed bitters' did not make a good impression on my palate nor endear me to the area. Towards the end of our training period we were granted a 48-hour pass and this enabled me to spend the weekend with my uncle, aunt and cousin Julia in Sutton Coldfield - one of the more salubrious suburbs of Birmingham. Besides the absolute luxury of a comfortable and decent bed, I enjoyed a trip to Stratford-on-Avon with Julia and her fiancé Ted. Back to camp for the final lap and the climax of the passing-out parade. With everyone bulled to the nines, we were put through our drills on the parade ground by our corporal instructors. It has to be said that the occasion generated a general sense of exhilaration, not only because we were relieved by the knowledge that the ordeal was nearly over and we had survived its rigours but also by a genuine sense of pride in our performance. This phenomenon of a final sense of euphoria figures as a theme in not a few memoirs, with even those most resentful of the whole experience admitting satisfaction at this final climax, similar perhaps to the euphoric feelings of a choir or a drama group following a public performance. The smiles on our faces in the group photograph taken after the passing-out parade look genuine and unforced.

I don't recall much in the way of celebration, everyone was too anxious to get away on well-earned leave. Assigned to our various trades, we were informed of our next posting. I was to become a radar operator and my next

Passing Out parade

destination was to be the radar school at RAF Worth Matravers in Dorset.

After home leave I travelled by train to Worth Matravers, a small station perched on the Dorset cliffs and close enough to the sound of crashing waves to imagine we had joined the navy. At a more clement time of the year Worth might well have been an idyllic posting. The area was breathtakingly beautiful, then as now popular with holidaymakers and walkers and within a few miles of resorts such as Swanage and Corfe dominated by its impressive castle. The village of Worth Matravers consisted of a small number of limestone cottages and farmhouses and boasted few amenities beyond a duck pond and a pub, the 'Square and Compass', renowned for its pints and pasties and welcome refuge for the personnel of the base. The snag, of course, was that January and February are not clement months. The weather was dry but cold and the wind came howling off the sea, making evening trips to the pub down the unlit lane an ordeal and even moving around the base uncomfortable. Our hut, needless to say, was uninsulated and draughty, having no heating beyond the central stove around which our small band of trainees would huddle when not in the classroom. We had been selected to be inducted into the mysteries of radar. We were to be operators of a particular system known as Gee, which was a navigational aid designed to improve the ability of bombing aircraft to locate and hit their targets with much greater accuracy than had been possible before the invention and development of the system. Aerial reconnaissance and subsequent research had revealed the shocking inaccuracy of Bomber Command especially in the early years of the war, after which precision bombing had largely been replaced by area bombing. The new system claimed to have improved accuracy to within a couple of hundred yards of chosen targets. Since by the middle 1950s there was not much bombing going on there was only a very limited demand for technicians and operators to man this particular system and hence only the small band of National Servicemen passed through the instructional centre at Worth Matravers. The course was scheduled to last no more than six or seven weeks and consisted mainly of lectures from a sole sergeant instructor. It was very like being back in school, especially for my fellow students who had presumably been chosen because they had studied science subjects, particularly physics, in their sixth-forms. Their attitude to the course content was therefore far more critical than mine since for me it was all new. Sometimes one or other of them would be bold enough to point out some inconsistency and it would then be forcibly pointed out that this was RAF physics which would override Ohm's or anyone else's law. Although only a small base with this somewhat limited function, Worth Matravers had a distinguished history as a centre for the early history and development of radar, the original base for a crucial Telecommunications Research Establishment (TRE). Many a boffin would have downed a pint and munched a pasty in the 'Square and Compass'. However, the TRE had been subsequently transferred to Malvern because Churchill had feared that Worth's proximity to the coast made it vulnerable to a German raid. It had nevertheless continued to function as part of that vital chain of radar stations which had played such a key role in the Battle of Britain. To much of this distinguished history we remained oblivious and nobody thought to enlighten us. Years later, when holidaying in the area, I revisited the site. All that remained was the camp foundations, though radar memorabilia are, I believe, on display in a museum in Swanage.

I have very little memory of my fellow students at Worth, except that they all knew more physics than I did. But I simply memorised what was presented to me by the instructor and therefore coped. One character I do remember well was generally known as 'the Hawk'. An ex-public-school boy, he showed complete indifference to rules and authority. On a number of occasions he raided the cookhouse after hours, climbing in through a window and returning with eggs and anything else that could be cooked on the hut's stove. Even after the break-ins were detected, Hawk dared to repeat the odd raid like a latter-day Raffles. When the cold became intense Hawk's solution was to lay his wardrobe flat, climb in wrapped in his bed clothes and shut the door. The corporal who rousted us out of bed in the mornings in the customary genteel manner would rat-a-tat-tat on the wardrobe door. Once, in response to a challenge, Hawk plunged into the icy water tank, there in case of fire, cutting his foot on some glass in the process. On trips to the pub he would stroll along with great-coat open, buttons undone, hat on back of head, indifferent to both cold and any reprimands that might come his way. Fortunately for the Hawk the discipline at Worth was very relaxed but I would be surprised to learn that his subsequent service history didn't include some guardhouse confinements along the way. His derring-do certainly provided much needed entertainment. Later I would encounter a similar case of public-school *sang froid*: their products seemed to fall into two categories, officer material or rebels. I left Worth Matravers a trained radar operator Gee H duly promoted, from AC2 to AC1. After a spell of leave I awaited to learn my next posting. It turned out to be Germany.

The aspiration of most National Servicemen was to see something of the world at government expense and given the shrinking but still global nature of the British footprint, this was not unrealistic. The large British presence in Germany made this the most likely destination. A foreign

posting carried the promise of extra pay but a typical governmental sleight of hand declared Germany to be a 'home' posting. By the stroke of the Treasury pen the North Sea was deemed not to exist. BAOR (the British Army of the Rhine) was about 50,000 strong, scattered across the former British zone of occupation in northern Germany in a number of bases stretching from the Dutch border in the West to the border of the Russian zone in the east. No longer

Roger outside bahnof

a zone of occupation, the British presence was as part of NATO (North Atlantic Treaty Organisation) established in 1949 and joined by the recently created Federal Republic of West Germany as a full member in 1955. The RAF also maintained a considerable presence both in support of the army and as a strategic force. The unit I was to join was part of the latter, 2nd TAF (Tactical Air Force), its principal weapon at the time being the Canberra bomber. I always considered the title BAOR revealing of the key British strategy, to retreat to the Rhine in the event of a Russian attack. Such a catastrophic event was not considered imminent but neither was it out of the question. The Cold War still dominated the minds of policy makers and it was to become more frigid in 1956 with the brutal suppression of the Hungarian uprising followed by the Suez crisis, during which Khrushchev threatened Britain with ballistic missiles. On the occasion that I found myself, fortunately briefly, stationed close to the Russian zone, the rumour was that everything static was mined in preparation for a classic British retreat. Life beside the Iron Curtain – a metaphor rather than a formidable barrier - except of course in Berlin – was edgy. Fortunately I was to spend the great majority of my time in Germany near to the Rhine and the Dutch border, where sleep at night came easier.

On 19 February 1956, after a few days leave, I was despatched to Germany. One of the paradoxes of being in the RAF was that, apart from aircrew, one rarely if ever flew, not even when transported to Germany (a 'home' posting of course). So it was that I joined a large body of men, mostly army, at Harwich where we embarked on a troopship headed for the Hook of Holland. This trip across the North Sea was notoriously unpleasant, especially in winter, and the ships employed had an evil reputation. Rumours abounded about mine, I think called the 'Lord Warden', having been salvaged at one point from the bottom of the ocean. It was all too believable. Men were stuffed into three-tiered bunks below decks and no facilities were provided since one was not expected to move until disembarked. There was nothing else to do but to hunker down in one's bunk and to try to keep one's stomach down. The crossing was rough, the ship heaved and the result was predictable. Once one man was sick it set off a chain reaction and soon the deck was awash with vomit. I remember that voyage as the worse experience of my time in the service and it may account for my lifelong reluctance to cruise. Seasickness is a horrid experience but recovery comes surprisingly quickly once back on dry land and it was a great relief to disembark and to board a train to one's designated destination. I was bound first to RAF Wildenrath and then on to RAF Butzweilerhof, a former Luftwaffe air base in the northern suburbs of Cologne, one of Germany's largest cities. There I was to join 124 Signals Unit, a small mobile force which was sheltering in Butz for the winter and was not at the time operational.

The weather struck me as exceptionally cold, perhaps because it was drier than I had previously experienced and the snow was several inches deep, thick socks and wellies the order of the day. We were fortunate to be holed up in a well-appointed base, our barracks heated and relatively comfortable. I joined five others in a small dormitory and was relieved to find myself in compatible company: the others were all National Servicemen, mostly ex-grammar school like myself, and trained as radar or radio operators. There was a friendly collective spirit, though newcomers would always be greeted with mock pity since they had longer to serve than anyone else. Advice such as 'get some in' or in tropical climes 'get your knees brown' was freely proffered, plus warnings about who among the hierarchy were to be avoided. The man I remember most among this band of brothers was a Scot, though to call him Jock would have been inappropriate since his dark hair, small moustache and sallow complexion proclaimed him to be Italian by origin. He was in fact a second-generation Glaswegian called Giovanni Renucci and the first Scots Nat I had ever encountered. He was very good-natured and our arguments were always laced with mockery and good humour. He could afford to be cheerful because he was on the last lap and would soon be heading back to Glasgow. Years later when I was visiting friends in that city, I looked up the name Renucci in the phone directory to find a string of Renuccis, mostly involved in the food business. I missed him in spite of his misguided political views, adopted I believe as much to tease his Anglo-Saxon comrades as out of conviction.

A core principal of military organisation is hierarchy. Our basic training had taught us that those blessed with a couple of chevrons on the arm, let alone pips on the shoulder, were endowed with arbitrary powers. This applied regardless of factors such as intelligence and competence. Circumstances where these were manifestly in inverse order were covered by the doctrine that it was the rank rather than the person holding it which commanded obedience. In basic training one had been obliged to suffer insults, however obscene, and intimidation with submissiveness, the charge of 'dumb insolence' existing to cover even a wordless show of dissent. This made friendships across the ranks not impossible but problematic and needing to be warily negotiated. Below the rank of corporal, rank scarcely intruded. Progress through the lesser ranks of Aircraftsman Second Class (AC2), Aircraftsman First Class (AC1), Leading Aircraftsman (LAC), Senior Aircraftsman (SAC) was largely a matter of time served with reasonable competence and a clean disciplinary record and carried little in the way of authority.

National Servicemen were very largely confined to these lower ranks, promotion to corporal being very rare. Those who aspired to be aircrew were almost invariably expected to sign on for a longer term than the two years of National Service. As National Servicemen in our unit composed of about thirty members we were a distinct and minority group. The great majority were regulars, older, more experienced and with a very different mindset. We were conscripts, often with a very jaundiced perception of the service. They were regulars whose choice it had been, often signed on for long periods. Not surprisingly, there were those who resented us as interlopers, even perhaps as subversives. Over the next eighteen months or so I got to know most members of the unit and to understand the sociometry. As operators of the radar and RT, the ones we gelled most easily with were the technically-qualified staff, under whose direction we worked. They were generally of a higher intelligence than the average. Preoccupied with the technical problems, they were largely indifferent to rank. Two men in particular seemed to me to stand out as key members of the unit, one a regular corporal, the other a National Serviceman.

Corporal Howard was well-read, clearly well-educated and from a middle-class social background and easy to converse with. He was married and living in married quarters but I was never invited to visit his home or to meet his wife. Semi-detached while we were at Goch, to which we moved after leaving Butzweilerhof, he would turn up at our site in his own car, a battered Borgwald, a now forgotten make subsumed into the Audi group. The other technician of note was one of us but with a difference marked by an upside-down single chevron on his arm, identifying him as a J/T, a Junior Technician. Hutchinson (Hutch) was a science graduate of Sheffield University who had been deferred and was therefore older than the average National Serviceman. He was amiable and mild-mannered and took no offence at the banter which his fussiness provoked. A popular song of the time was Harry Belafonte's *Banana Boat Song* and this was adapted so that when he entered the billet he would be greeted with a loud chorus of 'six-foot, seven-foot, eight-foot Hutch!' All taken in good part. It never occurred to Hutch that his upside-down stripe conferred anything in the way of seniority. The real cleavage in the unit was between those of us, whether regular or National Servicemen, who maintained and operated the equipment, and the other half of the unit, the mechanical section, drivers and driver-mechanics, who were responsible for maintaining and operating our extensive range of vehicles. Without exception they were regulars, most in for the long haul and generally of a lower-level of education. The height of their ambition was to attain the rank of corporal which would eventually come to those that waited. It was not uncommon to learn that some individuals amongst them came from unstable family backgrounds and had signed on in the RAF presumably for reasons of security and stability. While in base they had their own garaging and workshop and we saw very little of them. Several were married and living in married quarters. Unmarried corporals on base were allowed their own individual rooms, although some at Goch preferred to billet with the rest of us for social reasons, notably a small cross-eyed Mancunian, a General Duties corporal, who dominated the billet with his ebullience and somewhat warped sense of humour. Locked in a room alone Corporal Joe Hawley would have gone bonkers. Joe was always 'pulling rank' but with him it was clowning and meant precisely nothing. He exuded good nature and had a double-act going with another regular, a scouser called Vincent whose actual function in life I never fathomed.

If there were any NCOs to beware of they came from the mechanical section. A particularly unpleasant specimen was Bill Erskine, a squat and stocky Ulsterman, who always looked as if he had just crawled from under a diesel truck. Known to us as 'Bully Billy Foreskin', he would come into our billet at Butz at weekends, ostensibly to invite us to join him on expedition to Cologne's red-light district, knowing full well that we couldn't afford it even if so inclined. He did not, of course, offer to treat us but even if he had there would have been no takers.

There was always a certain apprehension about going into town and we tended to go in groups. This was especially so if going to a dance hall or an evening gathering when it was considered foolhardy to go alone. Although stories of assaults were more a matter of rumour than reality, and I don't recall anything untoward happening to members of my unit, caution was understandable. Cologne had been the target of Bomber Command's first 1000 bomber raid on 30 May 1942 and, in Max Hastings' account 'the city was left ablaze from end to end'. Hastings comments that 'no man who was ever there forgot this baptism at Cologne', least of all those who suffered under it and it would have been astonishing if none of the local inhabitants did not harbour bitter memories of RAF terror bombing. To rub it in, Bomber Command had returned to Cologne in March 1945, just a few weeks before Germany surrendered, the official report recording 61% of the target area destroyed. Thousands were killed and injured and some 45,000 people dehoused. The scarred cathedral, the central landmark in Cologne, was a stark remembrance of ghastly wartime experiences.

So, there was more than one reason why there were no takers for Bully Billy's invitation. His real purpose was to laud it over us and to enjoy 'pulling rank'. He took a particular dislike to me, perhaps because of 'the dumb insolence' that I made no attempt to disguise but reinforced when he learned that I was playing tennis with officers, one of whom had phoned the office and had mistaken me for a Pilot Officer. This, in Bully Billy's eyes, was a grave offence, violating his sense of hierarchy. He would regularly order me to get a haircut, an order I regularly ignored on the calculation that even he was not so stupid as to press a charge before the CO.

At the apex of the unit of course was the Commanding Officer before whom I was formally brought soon after arriving in Butz; cap in hand and stand to attention before ordered to stand easy. At the time he held the rank of Pilot Officer, the lowest commissioned rank, though he was later promoted to Flying Officer. I judged him to be in his early 40s and this suggested that he had risen through the ranks, probably having seen war service. He was unusual in that he was of Sri Lankan origin (as Ceylon became after independence in 1948). Tall and athletic, he was rumoured to have been an excellent hockey player. He was and remained an enigma and I never managed to have more than perfunctory conversation with him, indeed the opportunities to meet him were few because he was either married and lived in married quarters or quartered in the Officers' Mess, I never found out which. He would come and go in his own car, spurning the VW saloon intended for the CO's use. In one respect I was lucky in that he was keen on sports. I don't remember having the chance to tell him I was a tennis player but he somehow found this out and actively encouraged me, even at one time loaning me out to a base close to the Russian zone to play in a cup in which I had already been on the losing side with a different team. I had no difficulty gaining release to play in matches and tournaments and in the summer of 1957 I was allowed leave to return to the UK to play in the RAF Championships, in those days played on grass at Wimbledon. The opportunity to play tennis definitely made my time in Germany more congenial and widened my range of contacts.

During the CO's frequent absences, command devolved on Flight Sergeant Oakes, like the CO, a veteran. Flight was an easy-going Geordie, mercifully oblivious to any form of dress code or formality. Living in married quarters he, like the CO, was semi-detached and often absent. He would turn up in his Morris Minor, his well-worn battledress open, no beret and hitching up his trousers. He had a lot to say for himself but much of it for

Keep on trucking

effect, we knew that he relied on the 'techies' to run the show. Another member of the unit whom I didn't meet while we were hunkered down at Butz was the unit cook, a scrawny Scot who always looked to be in dire need of a solid meal. Like all Scots, he was 'Jock', as all Welshman were 'Taff' or 'Taffy'. When we were in base, Jock was consigned to cookhouse duties and this became something of a life-saver when at Goch we would often return late from the site and had to make do with left-overs. In the course of the evening, moved by our plaintive complaints of near-starvation, Jock would sneak across to the cookhouse and return with a heap of fried egg sandwiches, making him a very popular member of the unit. When we were under canvas Jock came into his own but he was no Gordon Ramsay.

Since, as is well known, the devil finds work for idle hands, while we were non-operational in Butzweilerhof, something had to be found to occupy us. I was loaned out to the fire service for a time and quite enjoyed tearing around the airfield in a fire engine though fortunately never required to extinguish anything. I also became part of a squad moving furniture in and out of married quarters, some of which were riddled with woodworm. The only constructive thing I did was to learn to drive, something required of all members of the unit. The vehicle chosen for my lessons was a lorry, a diesel-engined Magirus Deutz with at least half-a-dozen forward gears. My instructor was Corporal John Page, a tall and lean moustachioed hard-man. A man of very few words, he would put his feet up on the dashboard and read the *Beano* while I wrestled with the gears and progressed gingerly through the streets of Cologne, desperate to avoid the tramlines and of course pedestrians. After about eight hours and with my confidence growing I was pronounced qualified. Over the next eighteen months I would find myself behind the wheel of most of the unit's transport, including the heavy radar wagons. This, at least, was one skill I picked up over my two years – it is hard to think of any others.

There was also a sequel. When I returned to 'civvy street' with an international driving licence but not a British one, I discovered that my service qualification was not recognised and that I would be required to take a test. This struck me as an egregious case of British imperial *hauteur*. If Brits were at risk from my inadequate skills, what about the many thousands of Germans amongst whom I had careered, often in heavy lorries? I took my case to my local MP, by this time the Conservative Brigadier Jackie Smyth V.C. To his credit he put down a question in the House of Commons but, meeting with no response from the Minister of Transport, I was obliged to take a test in my reluctant father's Ford Popular. I also took a motor-cycle test while I was at it.

One of the most irritating aspects of those wasted weeks as an odd-job man at Butz was having to go on parade, thankfully for the very last time. Pay parade was a particularly galling experience. Given the paucity of comrades with names beginning with X, Y or Z. I would be among the last to leave the square. The pay was inadequate for much beyond topping up the skimpy cookhouse fare in the NAAFI. But the exchange rate of BAFFs, the Monopoly money in which we were paid, for marks was healthy, the equivalent of about twelve to the pound sterling. The German economy was beginning its impressive revival – the Wirkschaftwunder – and the upmarket shops in Cologne were beginning to display cameras and watches at attractive prices. I acquired a watch and an electric razor and have used a Braun ever since. We didn't have enough funds to afford much beyond the odd meal out, invariably an excellent steak or a schnitzel, and certainly not enough to join Bully Billy in his lecherous visits to the red-light district. In search of entertainment on the base I sought out the social centre run by the camp padre, a tubby middle-aged Anglican vicar with the rank of Wing Commander who laid on various social events alongside conducting services. He was rehearsing a cast to perform J.B. Priestley's *An Inspector Calls* and, since it offered some female company in the persons of ladies from married quarters, I allowed myself to be recruited, cast in the role of a police sergeant. The rehearsals were enjoyable but, alas, I never made the performance because, with the arrival of spring, 124 Signals Unit received its marching orders.

NS men about town

I also had hopes of learning German and my edition of *Teach Yourself German* went everywhere with me. But the Education Corps proved elusive and I never once connected with a formal class. Also disappointing was the very limited contact with local people, beyond a few orderlies working on the bases including some ex-soldiers. It was not so much that relations were bad or hostile as that they were wary and distant. I remember in a match against a local club, I received a ripple of applause when I served a double-fault, a unique event in my playing career, which I thought revealing of local feelings. The transition from occupiers to allies had not yet sunk in with many Germans. I very much regret that I would return from my stint in Germany knowing little more than pub deutsch. Education was not high on the War Office agenda.

It was with relief and a sense of excitement that that with the spring came the order to move. The time of odds and sods was over and I had no regrets other than being obliged to let down the padre. Our convoy out of Butz consisted of about a dozen vehicles – radar and RT wagons, trucks carrying the diesel generators, a couple of transporter lorries, a water bowser, a Land Rover and two Volkswagens, a saloon and a Combi for passengers. Our destination was Goch, which lay about 50 miles away in a north westerly direction. This was a small town in the district of Kleve, known to schoolchildren for its connection to Henry VIII's fourth wife, Anne of Cleeves. After her rapid divorce Anne did not return home but settled in London, outliving Henry and dying in Chelsea in 1557. Her reluctance to return tells one something about her home area. A mere fraction of the size of Cologne, Goch had suffered badly towards the end of the war as the Allies had smashed their way across the Rhine a short distance away. In February 1945, in a campaign curiously labelled Operation Veritable, it had suffered devastating aerial bombardment, swiftly followed by a ground attack with tanks and military occupation. Such events were well within the memory of most surviving locals and hardly made for good relations. British servicemen could find a much warmer welcome by crossing over the nearby Dutch border and what Goch lacked the likes of Billy Erskine could find in Nijmegen some 20 miles distant. I remember making an early visit to the cemetery at Arnhem where endless rows of British gravestones commemorated Operation Market Garden, surely the worst of Montgomery's follies. I made the trip on the back of John Page's motorbike and, although I wore pyjamas under my clothes I nearly froze to death. We stopped for ham and eggs, which the Dutch had the habit of undercooking and which I subsequently spewed up. A striking feature of the area was the number of temporary bridges erected by R.E.M.E. to replace those that had been destroyed by Allied bombing and artillery or by the retreating Wehrmacht. Goch had been kept as an army base but space was found for RAF124 Signals Unit, fortunately in a well-maintained barrack block. A well-established camp, there were decent facilities including a gym, a sickbay, tennis courts and a football pitch. We saw little of our army hosts, which was a matter of little regret, for in my observation wherever there was army there were parades, there was bull and there was a much greater accent on order and hierarchy than we had grown accustomed to. None of those things suited us one little bit. My sole contact was with a major who was one of the army contingent's senior officers who chose me to partner him in the camp tennis team. True to rank, he issued me with movement orders on court. He was, however, a decent old buffer and I was more amused than resentful.

The unit was once again bifurcated. 'The rude mechanicals' stayed on base, as did the RT, but the site for radar operation was established about ten miles away on rising forested ground not far from the larger town of Xanten, which had also been the scene of fierce fighting in 1944-5. In a clearing at the apex of the forest, marked by a wooden fire-watching tower, we laid down metal tracks on which the heavy wagons would stand, raised our masts, constructed a

Over 'ere and underfed. Author on radar truck

Our site in woods near Goch. Hutch taking the knee

latrine strictly according to War Office specifications, and used an old lorry top as the nucleus of a hut where we could shelter, brew up and sleep while on night-watch. We hoisted a sign proclaiming our credentials but no effort was made to fence the site or to prevent locals using the various tracks through the woods, which few did. Nor was there any suggestion that, even as the overnight guard, we should be armed and I can't remember ever feeling threatened in any way. The radar crew were driven up to the site each morning along largely empty flat country roads with cultivated fields on either side. With luck it would be aboard the VW Combi, if not in an uncomfortable lorry with benches along its sides. Our midday meals arrived from the base in aluminium cans, stacked in a frame with a candle at the base purporting to keep them hot. The result was stomach-churning. I can still recall with horror the sight of cold rice pudding streaked with black from the aluminium cans. Perhaps the worst feature of my time at Goch was undernourishment. Photos show me as skinnier than I have ever been before or since.

In the evening we would wait impatiently for the vehicle to deliver the night shift and to ferry us back to base. By the time we arrived, the cookhouse was either closed or closing and we had to make do with whatever the squaddies had left. Our loss inevitably was the NAAFI's gain. It was, I believe, a serious dereliction of duty on the part of the CO who, as far as I'm aware, made no attempt to rectify this problem. Those living in the Officers' or the Sergeants' mess or married quarters, of course, did not share our experience. Being in the woods all day was probably healthy physically but we mere radar operators were again woefully underemployed. The boffins spent the hours tinkering with the sets but except when we were operational, there was nothing for us to do. Operations, which involved bombers flying from bases in the UK and picking up our signals to guide them on to their targets, were expensive to mount and in those straitened times correspondingly infrequent. When they did occur, the deficiencies of our wartime equipment made successful transmission somewhat problematical and I remember a visit from 'top brass' to investigate some failure on our part. Our techies were always fiddling with valves, wires and soldering irons in heroic efforts to keep us operational. In our ample spare time we played a form of basketball and in cool or wet weather we sat in the hut reading or playing bridge, or simply gossiping. As far as radar operation was concerned, I felt less competent at the back-end of my service than I had been at the beginning. One was bound to ask oneself – was my service really necessary? Officialdom would have found justification in the acute crisis which erupted in late 1956. The nationalisation of the Suez canal by Nasser in July created a diplomatic furore which erupted into war in late November with an air and seaborne attack on Egypt by Britain and France, preceded by an Israeli assault across the Sinai desert. Ignominiously the offensive was halted within days by UN condemnation and US financial pressure and the Allied troops withdrawn. The Soviet dictator Nikita Khrushchev, whose tanks had so recently rolled into Budapest to crush the Hungarian uprising, widened the crisis by threatening a nuclear attack against the imperial aggressors. Tucked away in rural seclusion in Goch and out of touch with the British media, we had only the vaguest notion of what was going on. Rumours flew. Doubts were expressed about the capacity of our Meteor and of French Mirage jets to cope with Soviet Migs. Only Canberras could match them for altitude and were therefore being adapted for combat. More down to earth, we were all about to be vaccinated as a possible prelude to service in the Middle East. To most of us, the replacement of Eden by Macmillan was about as relevant as replacing Tweedledum with Tweedledee. By Christmas Nasser had prevailed and all had quietened down.

Our billet at Goch was more than twice as large as our room at Butz and housed all members of the unit other than those in married quarters or those corporals who chose to claim the privilege of a single room. The couple of corporals who preferred communal living, the irrepressible cross-eyed Joe Hawley and also the soft spoken and rather effeminate Corporal Wilson, who wouldn't have known how to 'pull rank' even if it had ever occurred to him, bunked with us. Luckily, I never again crossed swords with Bully Billy. We all got along together pretty well. This was a time when jazz and skiffle were very popular and a group of lads with guitar, washboard and tea-chest bass became popular performers in the NAAFI in the evenings. I acquired a record player and sent home for records (jazz greats, Chris Barber, Lonnie Donnegan) as well as books. My *Teach Yourself German* was always close at hand though progress lacked the stimulus or contact with the natives, of whom we saw very little beyond the odd visit to a Gastatte in the dull small town. Entertainment had to be largely on base and for me this meant tennis whenever the opportunity occurred. An early contact I made at the gym was with David Morgan, a public-school product that I would bracket with the 'Hawk' at Worth Matravers, both intent on doing their own thing and oblivious of authority. David would always appear dressed in a singlet and the dark trousers of a PE instructor, which the world took him to be. What his actual role and function were and what unit he belonged to remained a mystery. He was a tennis player who had represented the minor county of Bucks, his family home being in the affluent town of Amersham. Supremely confident of being selected as one of a small group sent to play in the RAF championships to be held at Munchen Gladbach, he reassured me that I too might make it and join him in the team. When the list was issued, I was on it and he was not.

With a magnificent *seigneurial* gesture, he arrived in my billet and dumped his sports bag on my bed, aware that I was short of kit. It included two bespoke rackets made for him by a small firm in the Finchley Road in London from Slazenger frames. I used them gratefully and with reasonable effect and subsequently used the same firm myself, before eventually switching to the ubiquitous Dunlop Maxply. The sequel to David's disappointment was his downfall. His cover was blown, I know not by whom, and it was revealed that he was not what he had bluffed the world into thinking he was. He was arrested and charged but I've no doubt he got off lightly since he could reasonably claim never to have declared himself to be a PE instructor, or, in spite of his lordly manner, an officer. He was returned to whatever job he was supposed to be doing, which as in so many cases, posed the question of whether it was ever necessary in the first place. On leave the following year I spent a weekend with him and his family in Amersham. He had somehow managed to survive without being sentenced to anything serious. Had he been in the army he would probably have faced a firing squad.

Of the men I met playing in matches and tournaments the two I remember most warmly were Malcolm Gibb and Adrian Stonebridge, both of whom had ambitions to make a career of tennis after finishing National Service. Malcolm was tall and physically powerful and seemed to have all the necessary attributes to go far in the game. Once released he took an early morning job in Borough Market humping sacks of potatoes, good for physical conditioning and leaving him free to play tournaments. After making a promising start his career seemed to fizzle out and I lost track of him. I remember visiting his home in Beckenham in Kent and meeting his tennis-playing family during the time we were both on leave in England in the summer of 1957 to play the RAF Championships at Wimbledon. Adrian lived in Sutton, Surrey, in a complex provided for families who had lost fathers in the war. Whereas Malcolm was taciturn, Adrian was outgoing and with a charming manner which he used to good effect in the course of a successful coaching career. Years later, after becoming British professional champion, he established a tennis ranch in Spain. It was a matter of great satisfaction to have defeated Adrian in the RAF championships at Munchen Gladbach in the summer of 1956 before being defeated myself. This pleasurable interlude included a brief flirtation with a pretty WAAF who was also competing. WAAFs were, of course, regulars and in my limited experience were often from unstable backgrounds in search of the stability that service life could offer. But each new day produced a new parting and I regret that Malcolm, Adrian and I were all scattered across North Rhine Westphalia. As for the WAAF, she was gone without a word the morning after the championships ended and it was back to Goch for me.

My time at Goch could be described as congenial monotony. Apart from the discomfort of to and froing to the site and the bad food situation, there was little to complain about. I got on well with most members of the unit and the atmosphere was relaxed and easy-going. However, we were after all a mobile unit and it occurred to someone set above us that we ought, like cookhouse gravy, to move around from time to time. The chronology escapes me but we had a number of excursions. One was a brief joint exercise with Americans which included an eye-opening stay at their base at Heidelberg. The contrasts were stark. Whereas we tinkered endlessly with our ageing and, no doubt in the eyes of our American counterparts, obsolete gear, they would simply scrap and replace anything malfunctioning. The contrast extended to living conditions. In their mess we were astonished to see fridges stacked with fruit-juice and cream and to be asked did we want an egg on that steak. I remember, with a sense of distaste, their latrines – a row of toilets with no privacy except for one with a vanity board reserved for NCOs. No hiding place there. There was also the eye-watering discrepancy in pay. We were generally shy of accepting the generous offers which came our way to be guests at evening entertainments. The hollowness of Harold Macmillan's assurance 'You've never had it so good' could not have been more starkly exposed.

Our mobile equipment also included tents and all the paraphernalia for life in the field. On the back of one photo I have is written Ludwigsburg, which is a town in south west Germany about a dozen miles from Stuttgart in the state of Baden Wurtemburg. Our time under canvas there would have been part of the operation mounted in conjunction with the Americans, the only occasion on which I had contact with our main allies in NATO. I have clearer memories of the expedition we made to Flensburg in Schleswig Holstein on the German-Danish border, where we established our camp close to the Baltic seashore. Having gone operational, we set up our tents and then had plenty of leisure time, with volleyball a popular occupation.

The weather was fine and any pretence of uniform was discarded for PE kit. The CO visited (I don't recall him taking up residence) and, a bit put out by the holiday-camp atmosphere, posted an order that ties were to be worn in the mess – a tent presided over by our skinny Glaswegian cook. The response of another Scot who was nearing release, was to appear at evening meal sporting a tie but otherwise stark naked. A cause of great hilarity and a story to tell his grandchildren. I don't recall any punishment though he may have received a bollocking! The sea-shore was rich in shellfish and one evening we had a barbecue of cockles and mussels cooked in vinegar and washed down with rum. The result for me was a near-death experience. I have never been so sick in all my life. My condition was not improved by Jock's suggested remedy of condensed milk and the lads were sufficiently alarmed to cart me off to the nearest military base where a medic took one sniff and turned away in disgust, proclaiming

Having a ball

me an alcoholic. His suggested remedy was copious draughts of water. Unfortunately, this was not my only brush with ill-health during the year, the other more serious and of far longer duration. Back in Goch I broke out in nasty patches of eczema, on my face, arms and chest. I put it down to poor nutrition over a prolonged period plus the odd dowsing in diesel oil when we refilled the generators from large, leaky barrels. I spent a few days in the sick-bay being lathered mainly with zinc ointment, only relieved by the company of a couple of orderlies who taught me phrases with which to address the pretty German nurse whose English was as deficient as my German. I subsequently learned that what I was being taught was obscene, which would at least help to explain why I was consistently given the cold shoulder. It soon became clear that whatever I was smothered with was ineffective and I was transferred to a military hospital at Wegberg, opened five years earlier near 2nd TAF's HQ at Munchen Gladbach. There I was tended by two young National Service doctors, commissioned after medical school, one of whom was a slim, attractive brunette known as Teezy Weezy. With the other young doctor I thumbed through medical textbooks. The application of a relatively new drug, hydrocortisone, seemed

Helping Jock with spud peeling

to work a miracle, but alas, had to be consistently reapplied. The small tubes would be with me for years to come. The inability to produce a cure raised the question of whether or not I should be returned to my unit and hints were dropped that I might qualify for early release and possibly some compensation. The thought of being pensioned off filled me with horror. To be invalided out of the service seemed to me to carry more than a hint of weakness, even disgrace. Besides, I had no job to go home to while the last six months of service was rewarded with the equivalent of a regular's pay, a big uplift financially. So I rejected the alternative and returned to my unit for what turned out to be the most enjoyable months of my service.

Presumably as part of NATO deployment and co-operation, in the early summer the unit moved to France. The plan was to set up our operation in the Vosges mountain range, not far from the ancient city of Colmar. Although this was years before NATO's difficulties with President de Gaulle's tantrums in the mid-1960s, as always dealing with the French came with complications. When our convoy crossed the French border we were blocked by French police, who had apparently not been notified of what they seemed to perceive as a hostile British invasion. After telephone calls and negotiations, we were allowed to proceed on our way. On this occasion our tents remained packed away and we were luxuriously accommodated in an auberge half way up the mountain on top of which we set up our signal masts. The auberge was run by a Madame and her daughter who would on occasion join in an evening of music, drinking and dancing. On this occasion I do remember the CO being present, presumably because there was no officers' mess in the near vicinity. Formerly one of the least useful members of the unit, I now experienced a significant upward shift in my status as the only French-speaker. I enjoyed deploying my A level French, in communicating with Madame, in negotiating with a local garage over minor repairs, in accompanying the bath run to the magnificent Roman baths in Colmar. One of my most interesting roles was to take a member of our transport section, Corporal Sam Bass, to a nearby French military base with acute stomach pains. At this time the French army was engaged in a vicious war in Algeria and morale among army conscripts was low and the spirit mutinous. The war cost 24,000 French lives and many more Algerian and nearly precipitated civil war in France. Conscripts were underpaid and their facilities poor and all this was reflected in the atmosphere. I returned the next day to find Bass desperate to leave and, once appendicitis had been ruled out, he was free to go. Apparently, he had been approached by conscripts for soap and razor blades.

My minor incursion into France did not go unnoticed: on my service record are the words 'fluent in French', nothing about my dexterity as a radar operator. My pleasant time in the Vosges was interrupted by the opportunity to play in the RAF championships, held annually on the superb grass courts of Wimbledon. In the absence of a flight, it entailed a train journey and the dreaded sea crossing, though this time calm and uneventful. My Wimbledon appearance was ignominious. Thanks to my brother's insistence that I should be best man at his Saturday wedding I found myself scratched from the singles. I covered my tracks by pleading a sprained ankle, though I doubt whether my CO was entirely convinced. In retaliation, 'Geordie' Oakes had reserved a job for me – to lay a telephone line from the radar site down the hill to the auberge, which entailed battling through some rough undergrowth, a last assertion of authority.

All servicemen, especially those serving overseas looked forward eagerly to the mail delivery, which usually came once a week. This was particularly so for those married or in a relationship. A *cliché* of those times, often employed by novelists, can be described in terms of 'Dear John' letters, in which the ending of a relationship would be solemnly conveyed and causing anguish. So there was always perhaps an element of apprehension when the mail arrived. In my case I had no female pining for my return, my only regular correspondent being my mother. Letters from wives and girlfriends would carry such initials on the back as SWALK (sealed with a loving kiss) and those going in the reverse direction might be marked with something more sexually explicit such as NORWICH. It wasn't until I was on the last lap in the summer of 1957 that a perfumed envelope began to be regularly dumped on my bed, supplementing my mother's weekly missive. The sender was a girl called Jacqui, a petite and pretty blonde hairdresser who lived with her mother in Forest Hill. She was a friend of my sister-in-law Ann and we had met at my brother's wedding. We dated a couple of times during my leave and she wrote regularly when I returned to the unit. In Ann's judgement she had 'set her cap at me' but, of course, the cap didn't fit. She was mature and out in the world, my world was yet unfledged and I had no intention of any permanent liaison. We met a few times after my demob but both recognised that it was an ephemeral relationship, sweet while it lasted but going nowhere. We parted amicably, but I remember her gratefully for those letters which spiced up my mail from home in my last few months in the service.

At last my time was up. After a few beers in the evening, I bid a fond farewell to those of my comrades who were sorry to see me go and set

off for home from the nearest railway station with the Hook of Holland my embarkation point (still no flights!). My ultimate destination was RAF Innsworth in Gloucestershire, where all the formalities of demobilisation were completed and I was transferred to the 'H' reserve until February 1964. I was a civilian once again. Dog-tired but elated.

Author on his way out

Reflections on National Service

Early manhood is a time for looking forward not back. Reflections come with age and time. I am minded of William Wordsworth's line, 'emotions reflected in tranquillity'. I have been fortunate in having years to reflect on those times and on the Labour government's decision to re-impose conscription less than two years after demobilising the five million men and women who had worn uniform at the end of WW2. This still strikes me as a momentous policy decision with far-reaching consequences for post-war society. Its reception tells us much more about the political culture and social attitudes of the time. Those most affected, of course, were the two million plus young men 'called up' and scattered across the globe from Aldershot to the Imjun river to serve the perceived global interests of their country, a mercifully small minority losing their lives or being injured in fighting nationalist insurgency in Malaya, Aden, Cyprus and Kenya and in the infinitely greater conflict with Communism in Korea where the Cold War turned hot. More might have lost their lives in Egypt in 1956 had not the assault to seize the Suez Canal from the Nasser regime been called off after a few days, a debacle which forced a reconsideration of military strategy leading to the running down of NS by the end of the decade. I was fortunate that I never had to fire a shot in anger, indeed never carried a rifle except during initial training or on the very few parades that I didn't manage to dodge. Nor did I ever feel threatened by the people among whom we were based, the great majority being neither hostile nor conspicuously friendly. The presence of some one million Russian soldiers in Soviet-dominated east Germany and central Europe no doubt reconciled the

'Wessies' to our presence, no longer occupiers but allies in NATO from 1955.

Most of the diaries and reminiscences of NS are understandably subjective. Recruits were divided unevenly between the three services, scattered around the globe, and trained in a wide variety of roles. Only initial training offered anything like a common experience. A common theme that emerges, however, is that of underemployment and boredom. A word that crops up regularly is 'skiving', a word somehow borrowed from a process in the leather trade which came to mean the practise of work-dodging, of appearing to be busy while in fact doing nothing. The search for 'a good skive' was almost universal. It doesn't take a Stakhanov to suggest that this was a very bad practice and I have often wondered whether it was not at the root of what economists have labelled as 'the British disease' of low productivity. If so, it has been a long-term consequence of NS, compounding the cost to the economy of withdrawing so many young men from productive employment.

The general sense of futility was a vacuum that the MoD failed to fill, leaving many young men with much the same sense as 'the Old Contemptibles' of 1914 as they marched, chanting 'we're 'ere because we're 'ere'. Again, skiving, though not a sense of underemployment, passed me by. I was fortunate enough to be attached to a small technical outfit where discipline was lax and nobody obliged us to do unnecessary tasks simply for the sake of it. I do regret that I left the RAF with few transferable skills other than the ability to drive large vintage trucks with crash gearboxes, since which time I have driven nothing as big as a Range Rover. I regret that I did not acquire fluency in German owing to the lack of available tuition and limited contact with local people. On the positive side, were there gains? Did NS make men of us as so many from the comfort of their lounge chairs suggested it would? I suppose there were things we could put into the column labelled personal development. I learned that status and competence did not necessarily coincide and not to judge a man (and occasionally a woman) by the stripes on their arm or the pips on the shoulder. I learned to live amicably alongside a variety of men from different backgrounds, educational experience, regional origins and to appreciate character and companionship. Psychologically I think it was important for me to serve. It would be an exaggeration to suggest that the Ward-Barker clan had a military tradition but from my maternal grandfather, a Guardsman in the Boer War, to my two uncles in the army in WW1, my uncle Reg a volunteer in the RAF in the 1920s and recalled together with two of my uncles and my father in WW2, an uncle commissioned from the ranks in the army, an aunt in the WRENs, bringing into the family circle a naval petty officer, and another aunt a Land Girl, service was hardly unfamiliar. Yet in family circles experiences were rarely discussed. My brother and I, both RAF, were next in line. Neither of us would ever have volunteered but it seemed like a natural progression and nothing to be alarmed about. One should remember, too, that the media of the time was saturated with wartime scenes and themes, whether in books, films, or radio programmes. Even children's comics featured strip cartoons figuring German soldiers exclaiming 'schweinhund' and 'Gott in Himmel'. War as a popular cultural theme continues to a surprising extent to echo down the years. The mythical escape of Adolf Hitler from his Berlin bunker in May 1945 and his afterlife in South America has by itself constituted a counterfactual industry, while books on war often either written or reviewed by the indefatigable Max Hastings, continue to roll off the press to fill the shelves at Waterstones, while no publication year is complete without at least a couple of Churchill biographies. In such a climate it is scarcely surprising that there was so little popular resistance to the Conscription Act of April 1947 while in Parliament only 78 Labour MPs voted against, some of them dismissed as fellow travellers sympathetic to the USSR and still harbouring the wartime myth of a benevolent 'Uncle Joe'.

Looking back on the Conscription Act in terms of policy-making, I consider it one of the most astonishing decisions of the post-war years. In July 1945 the Labour party won a landslide victory largely because it enthusiastically espoused the Beveridge dream of a welfare state and because Clem Atlee was not Winston Churchill, widely regarded in the social class to which I belonged as a 'warmonger' all too likely to involve a war-weary nation in further conflicts. Yet within two years of dismantling 'the warfare state' and demobilising the men and women in uniform in 1945, Attlee and Bevin were sounding a new call to arms. It would inevitably be at enormous cost to general welfare, the loss of productive capacity, a continued housing crisis and the drabness of so many of our towns and cities. The 'age of austerity' was inevitably prolonged, beyond even that suffered by defeated rival states as many travellers abroad observed. Could a near-bankrupt nation, the world's largest debtor, afford to clothe, feed, house and equip some two million young men, the last to serve finally being demobbed in May 1963? The minimal opposition to such a costly policy speaks volumes about the prevailing political culture. Deference, trust in authority, acceptance of social hierarchy were the norm. The justification set out by Clem and Ernie, which can be summed up as Cold War and Empire, provoked grumbling in the food queues but little active opposition.

These were largely the thoughts of later years. At the time I didn't question the general consensus and obeyed the call. For all the grumbling it wasn't really until after the Suez crisis in 1956 that critiques of the British foreign and imperial policies became more strident and 'the winds of change' began to blow. Even the Tory government persisted with NS for a few more years, though apparently being lenient with many who had been deferred since none of my college friends who graduated in 1960 ever received that buff envelope.

Undergraduate Days

My kitbag was lodged in my mother's airing cupboard, its contents fortunately never again required. My uniform, like many others, would one day be deployed on the local allotment. I had a few days to prepare for college. My preparations included a visit to the manager of the Upper Norwood branch of Barclays Bank to open an account and to receive unconditional overdraft facilities, the sort of confidence that has ensured my loyalty to Barclays ever since. He was of course aware that my father and uncle Sid were among his customers but, even so, such friendly and informal treatment seems regrettably to have been lost over the years. Financially I should have been in a favourable position. My Drapers' Company Arts Scholarship plus a supplementary state scholarship, on paper gave me a sum healthier than the local authority grant, but there was a snag. Grants were means-tested, on the ludicrous assumption that men of twenty plus who had served in the armed forces were somehow dependent on their fathers. Fortunately for him but not for me, my father had substantially increased his earnings by leaving *The Times* and working Saturday nights on *The Observer* and a couple of days for the Mirror Group. These were halcyon days for printers, days of 'whine and rises', the high wages accorded to newspaper printers reflecting the perishable nature of the product. Rupert Murdoch and the technical transformation of the print industry and the move from Dad's beloved Fleet Street to Wapping lay years ahead.

The chances of my father making up the level of my grant were precisely nil (hence the precaution of an overdraft). The alternative to moving into student hostel or digs was to stay at home in Roman Rise and this was what I decided to do. My mother was, undemonstratively, pleased to have me back, my father less so but in no way hostile. Toleration did not extend to lending me his car. The main snag was that Roman Rise was about a dozen miles from the Mile End Road in Stepney, east London, where Queen Mary College (QMC) was situated. The solution was a motorbike. I found a second-hand BSA Bantam with a disfiguring dent in the petrol tank which in no way affected its performance but did reduce the price. For the next three years my faithful Bantam proved robust enough to carry a pillion passenger when required on excursions and in holiday times. It was garaged under the back window of No. 27 under a waterproof sheet and, using a plank to navigate two small flights of steps, could be wheeled out into the road or back as required. It ran very economically on a gallon of petrol and a few shots of oil each week.

London University was a federal institution. Most of my trips were to Mile End but over time I was also able to attend lectures at UCL, at LSE and

Queen Mary College, University of London, 1950s

Senate House, University of London

at the Senate House, the University's HQ, where on Monday mornings an excellent series of lectures delivered by well-known dons from a variety of colleges was on offer. Senate House, which had been the designated HQ for Hitler's putative conquest, also had an excellent library. Near the British Museum in Malet Street, it was also close to the Student Union building with facilities including a pool in the basement. In my final year I also took a special subject under a distinguished historian, Professor Medlicott, at the LSE in the Aldwych, so I came to frequent parts of London hitherto unfamiliar.

Looking back on those days it is astonishing how easy it was to get around London and to park, as I did in Russell Square whenever I attended the Senate House. Imprinted on my mind is the route I took on most mornings in term time to QMC. Down Gipsy Hill and into salubrious Dulwich, the splendid college buildings on my left, duck pond on my right: through the village and into Denmark Hill, past King's College Hospital where my father died in 1965 and through Camberwell; up the Walworth Road to the bleak Elephant and Castle, then down Borough High Street and over London Bridge, turn right past the Monument, through the canyons of the City, on to Whitechapel and up the Mile End Road. Hold-ups were rare and the journey could be done comfortably in little over half-an-hour. When I arrived at QMC, the first task after parking the bike was to visit the basement washroom to wash the sooty deposit inevitable in a cross-London journey off my panda-like face and to stow my helmet and gear in a duffel bag. The first day I made this journey to QMC was the first day of term and the beginning of three years of undergraduate life in London.

Unlike other students who had been selected after interview, I had never before visited QMC until that first day. My first impressions were of a busy, vibrant place especially at lunch-time when students from the engineering, dental and medical faculties across the road with pent-up energies from their laboratory labours flooded into the refectory, common-room and bar. The History Department gave off no such vibrancy. My first impression was of a subdued and slightly apprehensive group of 'freshers' about thirty in all, almost equally divided between males and females. Conformity seemed to reign OK. All were smartly turned out, no gymslips but neat dresses and the odd three-piece suit in evidence on the male side. Only one other student, as far as I could make out, had done NS, and he in the navy. Otherwise all were fresh from school, both public and private, a fair cross-section of the less than 5% of the age group that in the late 1950s went on to University. Nor did I get the impression that the universities were desperately anxious to retain let alone expand the intake as they so obviously strive to do today. At our first gathering the Head of Department hinted that we were somewhat over-recruited and that there might have to be some adjustment after the first-year exams. He followed this up with the injunction that to read a book a day should be our standard and there was no hint that classes, lectures, seminars and tutorials were anything but compulsory. There was to be no 'skiving' here, that cultural inheritance from NS which would in my view contribute in no small part to the British economic tradition of low productivity.

The Head of Department, Professor S.T. Bindoff, was a magisterial figure: tall, craggy, with a slow and halting style of delivery and the habit of frequently consulting his pocket watch to ensure he didn't miss the next of his numerous committee meetings. Had I exchanged one CO for another and he rather more authoritative than the one I had left behind in Germany? Had I, after all, made a mistake in not seeking deferment? I felt uneasy, not a little uncomfortable and meeting other members of staff did not immediately change my mind set. It was a relatively small department, Bindoff and three other male lecturers, plus three assistant lecturers, Bindoff *protégés* whom he, a consummate networker, was steering towards university posts as they became vacant. His own scholarly productions were relatively meagre though he was highly influential in his field, his

Professor S.T. (Tim) Bindoff

Tudor England a standard text. Classes were reliably delivered, substantial and erudite in most cases but rarely topped off with Q&A, while the seminars tended to be stilted and inclined to morph into a further lecture. An earnest, industrious but conformist environment, the tone set from above. An example that comes to mind is that of a then assistant lecturer whom I later came to know as a Professor at Birmingham University, Eric Ives. Eric was a portly, rotund young man, busy and industrious, always dressed in a three-piece suit and revealing the suspenders which held up his socks when he sat down. Not for nothing was he nicknamed Alderman Ives. In short time I abandoned the jeans that suited my mode of transport to QMC, after I fancied that they had been subjected to a hard stare in a Bindoff seminar.

For a time I felt alienated, a hard-bitten, somewhat cynical observer of the scene, a Marlboro' man, a man alone. In time I began to discern the individuals emerging from the collective and there were two lecturers in particular that I felt had some perception that I wasn't quite the standard issue. Dr. Jack Scarisbrick was a scion of a Yorkshire Catholic gentry family and in the prime of life. Later Professor at the then still to be founded Warwick University. He was the Dept. heart-throb, urbane, slim, elegant and handsome with a beautifully modulated voice. I could have fallen for him myself had I been that way inclined! I had the feeling that, in seminar, he seemed to give me a sort of metaphorical wink which said, 'Yes. They are a bit callow, aren't they?' Probably pure imagination but a source of encouragement. I was not attracted to his subject area (a bit overloaded at QMC as elsewhere) but if I warmed to the Tudors at all it was down to Jack Scarisbrick. My second main source of solace was the specialist in modern political and diplomatic history, more up my street. If Scarisbrick was the heart-throb of the Dept. Dr. Robert (later Professor) Leslie was its *enfant terrible*. Proud of his Scottish links, he also loved to relay anecdotes about his time in tanks in WW2. His main publications were focussed on Poland in the nineteenth century and I remember him being thrilled by the award of an order by the Polish government, then of course Communist-dominated. Similarly rewarded was Paul Johnson, editor of the *New Statesman*, a bible of my youth since adolescence. (My first ever publication, if I dare call it that, was a letter whilst still a school boy reflecting on Hitler's missing genital, which shocked my mother. The next was an attack on Harold Wilson, not so much on account of his genitalia but rather his lack in that department). Naturally Leslie presented himself as pretty far left but I came to perceive him as more of a Whig than a Radical, prone to come to the defence of the Establishment in the face of any criticisms other than his own. This was more like it. His lectures, which he manifestly enjoyed delivering in his abrasive style, were stimulating and iconoclastic. He enjoyed contact with the students and plainly got a kick out of intimidating them, especially the women amongst us. He soon spotted me for a wrong 'un and in my first tutorial, when I offered him an argument he railed at me, calling me a 'Bolshie bastard' which in the circs I took to be a token of endearment. It was the beginning of a long, topsy-turvy relationship, like the curate's egg.

When I was studying diplomatic history under the suave and distinguished Professor William Medlicott at the LSE, Leslie would take me aside to check that I was getting the real deal and would sometimes vigorously chalk on his study window to reinforce his points. If I had a mentor at QMC it was Robert Leslie. He later became supervisor of my MA thesis, in the course of which I became acquainted with his wife and daughters. Our meetings usually took place in Chiswick pubs and once, memorably, at the Reform Club. But in truth, he had little interest in my choice of topic and when he was on a sabbatical Bindoff checked up on my progress and was shocked. I'm sure he would have administered a rebuke. Leslie enjoyed making sly comments about colleagues but was in awe of Bindoff and would never hear a derogatory word levelled at a man who no doubt not only valued but protected him in spite of his occasional peccadilloes. It was Bindoff who set the tone of the department and it was an earnest and industrious one. Though I gained nothing from Tim Bindoff's teaching, I came, like so many others to respect him highly for his integrity and his dedication to the welfare and interests of his students. He would play a considerable part in the ravelling of my career. That lay in the future.

What about the relations with my fellow students? I was, of course, not by nature a loner. Like many of the QMC students I was living at home and maintaining my local contacts, especially at West Norwood Lawn Tennis Club, but I was slow to be on much more than passing acquaintance with my fellow students. A breakthrough came however when a student with ambitions to join the committee of the very active Student Union as 'fresher' representative approached me to propose him at the hustings. On scant acquaintance he had picked me out. Flattering, but I fear I made a poor fist of it and he failed to get elected. His name was Richard Wheeler, he was on the surface very much like the conventional schoolboy that I saw as predominating among my 'fresher' colleagues. But, as our friendship developed, I discovered him to be tough and determinedly ambitious but in the nicest possible way. We became lifelong friends, he best man at my wedding in 1963 and I at his a couple of years after. Not having the most glittering of academic profiles, he always said that Bindoff had admitted him on the basis of his prowess as that rare thing, a legspin bowler. Perhaps, but that wise man would also have discerned the character beyond. A popular student, Dick opened the door to wider association and I was in danger of becoming integrated. Social wariness was diminishing while I got stuck into the essential purpose of my presence, studying history and exploiting the rich resources which QMC and the wider University had on offer.

Through my interest in sport, I began to make associations beyond the Dept. In the basement was a room with a couple of table tennis tables and I began to bring my Barna bat to college and play a few sets with a couple of students from the science faculty. I then captained the college team, entered the inter-University competition and we carried off the Caribbean Cup, up to that point in the possession of the Regent's Park Polytechnic with its corpus of Chinese students, then considered the main exponents of the art. This brought me modest fame, a write-up with photograph in the college magazine, *The Cub*. I played one game for the university team but clearly failed to make a mark for I was not again selected. In the Spring I entered for the LU tennis tournament to be held at the university sports ground at familiar Motspur Park. I did well enough to be selected for the university tennis team and would hold my place for the whole three undergraduate years, often playing third pair alongside a fellow QMC-ite, Bob Brown, though the affiliation of most members of the team over the period was UCL. I served under two captains, both from UCL, Bob (Bonte) Levine and Lawrie Strong, both fine players and well-organised leaders. Lawrie was the cousin of one of Bindoff's star pupils who went on to national fame, Sir Roy Strong. The fixture list was a strong one and included matches against county teams which took us away at weekends, sometimes including an overnight stay. We had a coveted annual fixture with the PUC (Paris Université Club). The French hammered us on their lamentably slow clay courts and we returned the favour on our grass at Motspur Park. Our weekend in Paris was notable for more than the tennis. We were arrested in a night-club when we were presented with an extortionate drinks bill which we refused to pay in spite of menaces. A potentially ugly incident was averted by the arrival of gendarmes, who rounded us up, packed us into a Renault van, drove us around the corner and let us out amid laughter. Arriving back in London distinctly the worse for wear I recall spending the night on the floor of one of the UCL team members in their hostel in Cartwright Gardens. But it was by no means all drinks and high jinks, we were a serious team and I particularly recall with pleasure participating in an overwhelming victory over Oxford University. During the winter the University paid for us to practice indoors and I recall once playing on a court next to several young Australians, one of whom turned out to be Rod Laver.

Meanwhile W.N.L.T.C remained my club and there I met and teamed up on occasions with a former New Zealand Davis Cup player who happened to be editor of *Lawn Tennis and Badminton*, one of two tennis magazines in circulation at that time. Always hungry for copy, Keith Dyer offered me a guinea a column for any reports and articles I could contribute. A few of my efforts were published. More satisfying than the relatively small sums this brought in was access to tournaments as a reporter and this included Wimbledon, where I met Lance Tingay of the *Daily Telegraph*, also a contributor of the magazine and at the time the *doyen* of tennis reporters. I also recall having tea with David Coleman, *Private Eye*'s 'Colemanballs'. I did of course also watch tennis, and equipped by Keith with a Leica took pictures, just one of which achieved publication. This was a photo of Pietrangeli, I believe still regarded as Italy's best ever player and ranked in 1959 by Lance Tingay number three in the world. When I snapped him in 1960 he had lost in five sets to Rod Laver in the semi-finals. The experience of that summer opened up the option of pursuing a career as a sports journalist. The reason why I didn't pursue it seriously now escapes me.

En route to Paris with partner Bob Brown

Practice, matches and time away, played havoc with my social life and led to the break-up with my first love, who was a secretary working in an office in Northumberland Avenue, off Trafalgar Square. Heather was a member of the Young Conservatives. An association which, in those days, served up the best parties, dances and other social events so that membership had no necessary political affiliations. Heather's weekends were precious to her and my frequent absences a justifiable cause of friction between us. I reluctantly decided to put an end to our relationship but found it painful and took time to get over it. The last time I met Heather was at her twenty-first birthday party at which it was clear she was well over me and had found solace in the arms of a young banker. You win some, you lose some. Subsequently I found a partner for the odd night out from among my fellow students and one in particular with whom I formed a pleasant relationship, but on my side entirely platonic. Shortly after we graduated she became engaged to and married one of the Department's Assistant Lecturers.

Because we were fully occupied with the university team Bob Brown and I were unavailable for selection to the college team, but in my second year I was persuaded by a friend doing a PhD in physics to join a mixed team which toured the west country. Not great tennis but great fun. I so enjoyed the area, Budleigh Salterton, Sidmouth and Exmouth, that I decided to stay on for the rest of the summer and signed on as a bus conductor for the Devon General. I found digs in Exeter where I made friends with a fellow boarder, a jobbing builder and a 'mod' with a suitably decorated and fashionable Vespa scooter on which we toured village pubs in free evenings. I returned ready for the autumn term with money in the bank, though not a lot.

Much of my social life was by now being spent in the company of my mate Wheeler and this included pottering down at holiday times to Southampton on my faithful Bantam to his parents' house and to their cottage on the coast at Mudeford. We enjoyed our various adventures but we never lost sight of our main purpose, to study and to graduate. Spring 1960 was the time to foreswear frivolities. One of my close friends, who went on to a highly successful academic career at Birmingham, Geneva, Cambridge and Austin Texas, Tony Hopkins, withdrew into a monkish existence, pleading a gammy leg. I never did this, trying to maintain a productive work/leisure balance. It worked pretty well.

In the early summer of 1960 the doors of LU's vast examination halls swung open. London University History students faced ten three-hour papers in the course of a week, which I considered a particularly gruelling ordeal for female students to face and leaving us all drained and apprehensively waiting for the results which would be posted at Senate House. In the meantime, Bindoff found me a job checking overseas GCE papers in Senate House. I recall one from the West Indies blank except for an accomplished drawing of the car Genevieve from the 1953 comedy film. In place of the number plate was a sign reading 'please pass'. He didn't.

I was well pleased with my 2:1 (Upper Second) which was considered a good result at a time when Firsts were as rare as hen's teeth and most students ended up with a 2:2. I was less pleased to be told informally, I think by Leslie, that I had come measurably close to a First. Leslie told me I may have been let down by a poor language paper, for which two languages had been required and in which I had been baffled by a passage of obscure medieval Latin, a language in which I had had no tuition since the fifth form at Tenison's. In retrospect perhaps I should have tried German, though I doubt whether my pub deutsch would have served me better than Latin. Fortunes can be determined by small margins. My result was enough to persuade me that my future lay in teaching and that I should continue to pursue an academic career. Not until 15 March 1961 were we presented with our degree certificates, handsome vellum scrolls, in an impressive ceremony at the Royal Albert Hall. The presentation was by LU's Chancellor, Queen Elizabeth the Queen Mother, performing one of the least enviable of formal engagements with smiling aplomb. The band of the Welsh Guards provided musical accompaniment.

I look back at my time at QMC with gratitude. Not the most glamorous of History Departments but from Bindoff down it could boast a sound record of academic achievement. Yet there was also a lighter side. I recall for instance a residential study period at Beatrice Webb House in Windsor Great Park. Hopkins, Wheeler and I for a time ran the departmental History Society, me in the far from onerous role of treasurer, and we arranged the odd event such as a Chinese meal in the Commercial Road where I remember Bindoff joining us. My references confirm my conversion from cynical National Serviceman to fully integrated student. One from a rather surprising source, since my laboured essays in her subject area had consistently failed to impress. Helena M. Chew, our saintly medievalist, described me in glowing terms and closed with 'his relations with his fellow students were excellent and he has been described to me as thoroughly clubbable'. Crikey, did she mean me? *Per ardua ad astra.*

Learning to Teach

With a decent degree result on my CV and with a strong sense that I wished to continue studying my subject in some manner, I now had to plan for the future. I had discarded notions of journalism. In some ways, and if this was commonly felt it was a fault of the system, I felt disqualified from seeking a career in commerce or industry. Civil service exams were worth considering but the Department I would aspire to after my special studies of diplomacy, the Foreign Office, had a reputation for being notoriously elitist and I calculated that without connections I would stand no chance. The idea of postgraduate research had appeal but the road to a Ph.D. in history was a solitary and penurious one, seldom taking less than four years and, given the size of Universities at that time, carrying no guarantee of employment at the end. My thoughts turned to teaching. My subject knowledge could be put to good use and my love of sports might provide an additional dimension. I liked children and the idea of the classroom held no fears. I decided to test the waters by using my new-found degree status to apply to do supply teaching in the few weeks remaining between graduating and the end of the school term. I was taken on by Lambeth and sent to a girls' secondary modern school in Camberwell, by no means one of the borough's more salubrious districts. It was a case of a square peg in a round hole and what to do with me must have posed a conundrum for the redoubtable headmistress. She decided that I would do least harm if she put me in charge of a class of school-leavers serving out their last few weeks. Many of them, I soon learned, were already wise to the ways of the world, helping out in one-parent families and looking after siblings, a frequent excuse for lateness. They were now looking forward to earning a wage, perhaps behind a counter in Woolworths, serving on the many market stalls that lined the Walworth Road or, the favourite, working in a hairdressing salon. In this context, I recall the headmistress's words at the conclusion of a school assembly, 'Remember girls, your hair is your crowning glory'. Any apprehensions I felt were soon dispelled. The girls were apathetic but placid and not unfriendly and I had no discipline problems. What to teach them? The most sensible approach seemed to be history through story. What about famous women – Boadicea, Joan of Arc, Mary Queen of Scots, Marie-Antoinette? Maybe Nell Gwyn or Wallis Simpson might be more appropriate, though I suspect the fashionable hairdresser Teezy-Weezy would have stirred greater interest. It didn't seem to matter much. One piece of egregious flattery, not unappreciated, came from a doe-eyed blonde who generally parked herself in the front row. 'You just talk sir, you talk so nicely'. My confidence growing, I could relax and get to know these girls as individuals, after all they were little different from those I had more than rubbed shoulders with on Norwood Park and the Rec. One of the younger teachers on staff invited me to a Saturday night party in her flat near Denmark Hill. There can be few occasions more depressing than an undiluted gathering of teachers, conversation inevitably turning to the iniquities of the children, the disorganisation of the school and the general harassment they all felt in the job. Probably all justified but of little concern to one such as myself who was simply passing through, bound it was to be hoped, for better things. However, you have to start somewhere and for me it was doing my best to manage a class of very worldly and decidedly unintellectual but down-to-earth girls in Camberwell. I wonder if there were any hairdressers in the area who remembered in the dim and distant past a young teacher who talked so nicely and was apparently obsessed by fallen women?

It was not at that time a legal requirement for teachers to hold a professional qualification, though it was increasingly becoming the norm in state schools, much less so in private. It therefore seemed sensible to consider a one-year course on offer at most University Departments of

Education, for a Post-graduate Certificate of Education (PGCE). I cannot now recall why Dick Wheeler and I decided to apply to the Cambridge Department, though I suspect 'the invisible hand' of Professor Bindoff. We were duly accepted but it was a rule that all Cambridge students must be members of a College. The instruction came from above: 'Apply to King's'. King's College had the reputation of being the most elite of Cambridge colleges, something of a finishing school for Eton and a haunt of eccentric scholars with dubious sex lives. What we didn't know at the time was that QMC had been evacuated to Cambridge during the war and been generously accommodated by King's. This connection was maintained and Bindoff was unlikely not to have cultivated it in the interest of QMC students. One of his former students, John Nightingale, was *in situ* at the time working for a Ph.D. in medieval studies. Ward and Wheeler were now about to join him.

Admission to the Cambridge Department came with the instruction to spend time before the start of the university term gaining some school experience. Educational policy-making is a perennial cockpit of ideological conflict and at the time arguments over the efficacy of selection and the grammar school vs. comprehensive were ongoing. In London the supporters of comprehensivisation seemed to be winning the argument. London had opened its first comprehensive, Kidbrooke with 2,000 pupils in 1954, quickly followed by others. A recent addition was situated in Forest Hill not far from my home in Norwood and I asked to join the staff unpaid for the purpose of observation. My overall impression was none too favourable: there seemed to be a lot of movement around the school, especially at lesson change-over times and I wondered how long it would take for children coming up from their much smaller junior schools to settle in. Also, whether vital relationships between individual teachers and individual pupils might be hampered by the numbers involved. As a Radical in politics, I had no objection to the comprehensive principle but I felt that it was unfortunate that it should be associated with large pupil numbers, justified by its proponents in terms of economies of scale but posing management and organisational problems. At lunch one day I commented

to the teacher I was shadowing that I hadn't met the Head, to be told that
he was sitting at the next table. The negative impression I formed in what
was admittedly a brief experience was not without influence in the shaping
of my ideas about educational structures and the choices I would make in
my own future career.

With these two brief and contrasting school experiences behind me
it was time to become a pupil myself once more. My well-worn Bantam
was tucked away under its ex-MoD waterproof sheet under the window
in the back garden and I took the train to Cambridge. It was with a sense
of excitement and no little trepidation that I passed through the gates
of King's for the first time and registered my arrival at the Porter's Lodge.
The beauty of the campus, the elegance of its buildings and above all the
iconic chapel so often used in the media as a synonym for Cambridge itself,
couldn't help but make an instant impression. Whether one entered King's
from the front or the back, across the bridge over the Cam, that feeling
of entering a very special place never faded. Not only the chapel but the
Great Hall too had an aura, with the portraits of great figures from the
several centuries of its past adorning its walls, statesmen and scholars. One
could hardly help feeling humble and insignificant in such a setting and
one wondered how we interlopers from the East End would be received.
Such fears did not take long to be allayed. I remember being amused on
the first occasion when, at the end of a feast in the Great Hall, the toast
was proposed of 'Floreat Etona, Floreat QMC'. Somewhat incongruous but
sincere. We had been accepted by King's and were treated, as far as I could
discern, no differently from any other Kingsmen and this inclusive identity
would be sustained through life. Dick and I did not lodge in college and our
tuition took place in the Department of Education but the college served
as our base; the library if one chose to work there and the post-graduate
room, a comfy place to relax and to make the acquaintance of fellow
graduates and sometimes to attend inspiring talks from scholars at the
cutting edge. There was also the Buttery, where one could easily run up an
alarming bill and the Refectory if one needed a main meal. There were also
opportunities to meet and perhaps converse with well-known intellectuals.

The Provost, Noel Annan, was part-philosopher, part-sociologist and an entertaining speaker. E.M. Forster was in residence, living with his male partner. I remember a somewhat hair-raising tour of the chapel roof led by John Saltmarsh, Fellow and historian of Cambridge. Evensong in the chapel was a spiritual experience even for an agnostic like me. Candlelight, the splendid choir, the Rubens masterpiece above the altar, all created an incomparable aura.

The delights of that year were not confined to the College. Rather than seek lodgings in college or digs in the town, Dick and I decided to apply for Madingley Hall, a fabulous Tudor mansion owned by the university and in use as a graduate hostel and place of residence for visiting scholars. The Hall was situated about three miles outside Cambridge, a pleasant trip along the Madingley Road by bicycle. Madingley was expensive compared to the alternatives but very good value in relation to what it had to offer. I trusted that the bill would not cause my bank manager too much uneasiness and, indeed, there was no complaint from that quarter. The Hall itself was elegant, well-furnished and set in extensive and beautifully-maintained grounds. In one corner, as if in disgrace, was a small lake and hidden away on a bank stood a statue of Prince Albert, who had died of pneumonia following a visit to his errant son Bertie, the future King Edward VII. The statue had originally stood in the centre of Cambridge but, Prince Albert never having been a popular figure, had eventually been exiled to Madingley. Below the Hall on the main road and next to the village cricket pitch was a conveniently situated pub. My bed-sit was in a modern block facing the courtyard, comfortable and well-furnished with wardrobe, cupboard space, desk and bookcase. If there was a highlight at Madingley it was the evening meal, served in the spacious dining hall by maids and presided over by the Warden, Dr. F.R. Salter, who would sit at the high table with any visiting guests. The food was excellent and far beyond the range ever served up at home let alone the miserable offerings of my NS days. The company was stimulating. As well as post-graduate students doing research there were visiting foreign scholars, including from the US, Canada and South Africa. My near neighbours included Patrick Bateson, later to become Provost of King's and Keith Hopkins, later to be Vice-Provost. Patrick Bateson, a tall elegant figure with a bit of a stammer, was pursuing research into animal behaviour and insisted one day that I should give him a hand with his chickens at the Research Centre. Hopkins was a classical scholar, researching a thesis on social mobility in the Byzantine Empire. He was lively and mischievous and loved to regale visitors with tales of eunuchs who seem to have figured prominently in his research. As a neighbour he was very undesirable, living on the floor above me and addicted to playing Beethoven at full blast late into the night. Complaints would be brushed aside with *insouciant* charm, often with his hand in my biscuit tin. He went on to become a Professor of Sociology at Brunel before returning to his *alma mater*. One of his pleasures was to devise ways of annoying Warden Salter. This was not a terribly difficult thing to do since Salter was an old-fashioned, tweedy Edwardian with a distinctly conventional idea of how ladies and gentlemen should behave. Arriving late for the evening meal, for instance, verged on a capital crime. A retired Fellow of Magdalene College he had written a book on Karl Marx in the early 1920s and was rumoured to have stood for Parliament as a Labour candidate in his younger days. If so, there was little of the progressive remaining. His idea of acceptable behaviour certainly precluded dating the maids, who were German, obviously from good families and working to improve their English. There was no overt rule forbidding such liaisons but it hovered unspoken in the background. Given the imbalance of the sexes in Cambridge and the fact that the German maids were the most attractive women for miles around, this was clearly a non-rule to be evaded. Exploiting my encyclopaedic knowledge of their country and of their native language, I managed to develop a friendship with Ilsa, a well-built and attractive if rather solemn blonde. We would arrange to meet outside The Hall gates for a gentle stroll through the village or past the American cemetery and, if I happened to be 'at home' in the afternoon, there might be a discreet tap on my door. This pleasant flirtation, however, came to an abrupt end. When I returned to Madingley after a lengthy teaching practice in the early weeks of the spring term I found myself cold-shouldered. Ilsa's friend Dagmar explained that she was upset that so many weeks had gone by without so much as a postcard. She had evidently taken our relationship more seriously than I had. With my reputation among the German maids now *schlamm*, I was obliged to do without female company for the rest of my time at Cambridge – a case of 'Aufwiedersehen pet'. However, it was time to concentrate fully on my studies and to prepare for exams.

Although we were assigned a personal tutor at King's, this was a mere formality and effectively our tutor was the man who marshalled the small group of historians at the Department of Education and who delivered the lectures on the History of Education, Dr. J.P.C Roach. Dr. Roach, Fellow of Corpus Christi, was a bachelor aged about 40 but looking somewhat older, having been an officer in the Indian army during the war and, if rumours were true, had spent time as a prisoner of the Japanese, something about which I never felt able to ask him. He was short, sturdily built, with a rather husky voice and a habit of snorting and appearing to be trying to chew the end of his moustache. He was amiable but, like Salter, very conventional and he clearly arrived at the view that, unlike my friend Wheeler, I had a few rough edges to be knocked off. I remember him ticking me off for my very casual reply to an invitation to sherry and instructing me on how to respond correctly in future. In spite of his rather obvious reservations about me, our relations were pretty amicable. To me he seemed to be the very model of a Cambridge don but some years later he surprised me by moving from Cambridge to Sheffield, becoming the second Professor in the University's Department of Education. He settled happily in Sheffield and spent the rest of his life there, living until the ripe old age of 95 and dying in 2015. We kept in touch over the years and I remember him visiting me in Birmingham at a time when my wife was in hospital having our second child and I was caring for our two-year-old son, with John much impressed by my child-rearing skills, something which – as I know he regretted – had passed him by. But I don't think I ever overcame his reservations about me and for my part I felt he let me down on occasions. When I published my first book, he told me rather cruelly that he already had several books on Birmingham and wouldn't be buying a copy. Then there was the occasion when he was a member of a selection panel for a job which I had applied for and told me after the interviews that I had done well but had come second and that he had remained neutral because of our relationship. Hardly the Bindoff spirit. But reverting to our Cambridge days, it was John who placed the history students in schools for the lengthy second term teaching practice. He sent my friend Dick Wheeler to Charterhouse, a top public school but when I suggested that the logic of being at King's was to send me to Eton he turned sceptical and despatched me to Chigwell in Essex, a comparatively minor public school. This I took to be a rebuff, evidence of his doubts about my Establishment credentials. While I was happy at Chigwell, I regretted that he had denied me the chance to sample that most celebrated and also most maligned of schools.

I was treated very well at Chigwell, a school which included a boarding department for children from the age of four upwards and was situated on a site of about a hundred acres beside the main road which ran through Chigwell village. Opposite was a fine old inn, the King's Head. I was given a bed-sit in the Headmaster's house where another teacher, Peter Croft, also lodged. My room was old-fashioned but comfy, heated by a wheezy old gas fire beloved by the family's overweight dachshund, who in the evenings would lay belly-up in front of it snoring and farting. The Head was hospitable and generally undemanding, except when on occasions he would knock on my door first thing in the morning to ask me to take class X or class Y because he had something on outside the school. Unfortunately for me it usually involved a Bible reading – hardly my cup of tea. His wife was easy-going and unconventional and, in general, the house was something of a shambles. A story went the rounds that the village constable, finding the front door open one night, entered the house and assumed from the state of it that it had been burgled. The Head came down in his pyjamas to assure the PC that everything was as normal. The head of history, to whom I was assigned, was solicitous and conscientious but excessively uptight and there were few moments of humour and certainly not ribaldry in his classes. He was married to a Swiss lady, an excellent cook, who told me that he remained totally silent during the holidays in order to restore his voice. I later learned that she had been tragically killed in a road accident. I got on well with the boys, teaching some English as well as History, though my discipline fell below the standards demanded by my fellow house-mate, Peter Croft, who would have made a good adjutant in a Guards regiment. But he softened and generously treated me to a number of meals and drinks in the King's Head. The atmosphere in the school with the tone set from the top was benign, but I couldn't help but feel sorry for some of the prep school children. I came to the conclusion that boarding at an early age either made or marred. Some young children simply needed their mothers and not the care, however well-intentioned, of their matron.

A notable acquisition at this time and what turned out to be a rash purchase was my first car. In one of my classes were twins whose father owned a local garage. Through the boys I enquired if he had any cars going cheap. At that time large cars cost far less than smaller more economical ones and he sent me a message to say he had a Rover that he would let me have for £100. The problem, of course, was that I didn't have £100 and nor did I feel able to approach my long-suffering Barclays bank manager. Without much in the way of hope, I asked my father to lend me the money and that canny man said he would lend me £75. When I relayed this message to my garage-owner-parent, he agreed to let me have the car at that price as my father had suspected that he might. The Rover was about a dozen years old with faded but impressive quality, including green leather upholstery and a walnut dash with fitted tool-kit. A real limousine but, of course, totally unsuitable. I managed only about 20 miles to the gallon and any repairs were going to need specialist work at specialist prices. However, it was a pleasure to behold John Roach's face when he first spotted me at the wheel. After Chigwell, it was back to Cambridge. During the summer term I played some tennis, turning out for the King's College team. On first arriving at Cambridge I had been invited to join the University Tennis Club based at Fenners. What I found was a group being formed with the annual blood match with Oxford already in mind. The routine included some basic physiology and, horror of horrors, circuit training. The price of adding a 'Blue' to the 'Purple' I had won at UL was set too high and I soon absented myself. I finally blotted my copy book in the summer term by inviting a young Fellow of King's, John Goldthorpe, to have a knock, to be told that as a non-member he was not entitled to play at Fenners so we repaired to a college court. John was, I believe, the first sociologist to be appointed to a Cambridge University Fellowship and went on to be a distinguished Professor and a leader in his field. Following that rebuff I confined myself to inter-college tennis and I remember partnering a Sikh in his final year, Rajah Singh, whose last words to me were 'If you're ever in New Delhi, look me up'. But my main preoccupation had to be with my studies. I laboured without much joy through classes on the standard educational topics of sociology, psychology and philosophy, the latter taught very sparingly by Dr. Thouless, a man of few words who obviously felt that it was sufficient for us to read his book, *Straight and Crooked Thinking*. More enjoyable were John Roach's history lectures. I also recall elocution sessions with a posh lady speech specialist with Rupert Brooke's *Grantchester* a favoured practice piece. Students were invited to present a dissertation through this was not compulsory and I opted to research a nineteenth century report on the state of popular education, the Newcastle Commission. John Nightingale was one of my neighbours at Madingley working on his Ph.D. and would in time become a Fellow of Magdelene College Oxford. He kindly designed a cover with the title in impeccable medieval script. The dissertation earned a Commendation. I also achieved Distinction in the History of Education.

Job done. I returned home to Roman Rise with a freshly-minted PGCE and a far from freshly-minted Rover that I couldn't afford to run. This problem was relieved by executing a judicious swap. My technically-skilled brother had restored a Hillman coupé of indeterminable age and pedigree and rebuilt the engine. However, it had soft and probably worn-out springing and would roll alarmingly around corners, which my sister-in-law Ann, pregnant with her second child, found most uncomfortable. The Rover would be ideal for her condition and the Hillman for mine. It provided economical motoring and between us we could handle most of its mechanical problems except for the cable brakes which proved impossible to balance so that the driver had to compensate for the resultant veer when braking. Fortunately there was at that time no MoT test, otherwise the Hillman would soon have been parked on the scrap heap instead of providing me with two years of swinging and veering motoring, fortunately accident-free. The steep slope on which Roman Rise had been built was a distinct asset for starting the engine when all else failed. I resumed my social life, joining Dulwich tennis club which, unlike my old club W.N.L.T.A, had grass courts but I never really felt at home there and confined myself to social rather than competitive tennis.

But that summer I had other things than tennis on my mind. I was unemployed and it was time to think about earning a living. The main source of information about teacher vacancies was the *TES* (Times Educational Supplement). As I searched its pages my initial inclination was to focus on private schools in rural settings, probably with the model of Chigwell in mind and in the hope of accommodation being offered. The response was disillusioning and I don't recall being called for a single interview. The conclusion seemed fairly obvious: private schools preferred their staff to have been privately educated and to have Oxbridge degrees. *In extremis*, given the shortage of maths and science teachers, a London degree might just be acceptable. Class of degree and possession or not of a professional qualification seemed to be secondary considerations. Information I was receiving about the fortunes of others tended to confirm these impressions and I'm sure John Goldthorpe could have provided statistical data to prove the point. To some extent I felt I had allowed myself to have been misled by the easy acceptance I had received at King's. Social distinction ruled OK and my social profile simply didn't fit. I was obliged to shift my sights to the state sector and, preferring not to go into the comprehensive system, where better to look than to the London grammars where my social profile and qualifications seemed likely to be better received. It was soon apparent that there was no great shortage of history teachers but an advert which caught my eye was tempting. It was for a history graduate able to teach some junior school French at Battersea Grammar School in Abbotswood Road, Streatham. This was not entirely ideal. The subsidiary subjects which I offered and had received some training in as well as inclination were English and PE. However I felt I should be capable of teaching French beginners. The location of BGS could not have been more convenient, only some two miles from home and almost on the 137 bus route which went past Roman Rise bound for Streatham Hill station, situated within a few hundred yards of the school. The school itself, a 1930s building, was located in its own grounds and adjacent to the open spaces of Tooting Common, so much in contrast to the cramped site of my old school and no doubt helping to account for BGS's strong sporting reputation. I sent in my application and was interviewed by the Headmaster, Dr. Walter Langford CBE. It seemed a mere formality and he paid me the compliment of suggesting I was over-qualified for the post on offer. I would be the third history master on the staff and therefore could expect to teach mainly junior classes but he assured me that, once settled in, I would be given a share of senior classes. On that basis, I accepted the job. It had obvious advantages. It was an area I knew well and I could live at home, at least long enough to repair my finances and accumulate a decent wardrobe in an era in which teachers were expected to wear suits and indeed, in grammar schools, gowns and not look as if they were part of the retreat from Moscow as so many do today. And, incidentally, I had an excellent tailor, Ray Reakes, in Upper Norwood who made excellent suits, etc. at reasonable prices.

Batersea Grammar School

The structures and the routines at BGS all seemed familiar and I had no difficulty settling in. I became form master to a class of newbies, bright cheerful boys, keen and enthusiastic. Most of my teaching was confined to the lower school, my most senior class being in the fourth form. Above that level the senior history master, Clark, did the lion's share of the teaching with a lesser share going to the second history master, an ex-naval officer, Chris Everest. Clark was elderly, opinionated and something of a loner in the staff-room. Among the boys he had a reputation for eccentricity, though not of a humorous variety. I didn't find it easy to relate to him but he largely left me to my own devices. The only advice I remember, prompted by Everest's difficulties in coping with a sick wife, was to be sure to marry a woman 'sound in wind and limb'. I soon made friendships across the staff. I got to know Alex, a fifty-something PE master, as a result of being team mates in the Old Grammarian's third XI, after I had been introduced to the OGs by the master who organised the school football, Colin Bray, himself a good performer who turned out for the OGs first team. I also took over the coaching of a junior XI which involved some after-school practice and matches on Saturday mornings. OG matches were mostly played on public pitches on the local commons, with a few drinks afterwards, often in

All my sons. BGS 2nd XI

the Surrey Tavern. Old Boys delighted in telling stories about their years at the school, with Clark's oddities featuring prominently in their memories.

The referee's a …

The woodwork master, John Foan, became a friend and I met up socially with him and his fiancé Joyce from time to time. I also recall a talented young art master, who joined the staff at the same time as I did. His ambition was to be a full-time potter and he was beginning to sell some of his work to a leading West End store. I still have on display a painting in the style of Braque that he gave me. But my fondest memory is of John Edmunds, a part-time English teacher and accomplished linguist fluent in both French and Russian. John was making his way in TV, understudying his close friend and principal BBC announcer Richard Baker and later moving on to ATV. Welsh by origin, John was dark and handsome, always elegantly dressed, relaxed and oozing charm and aptly known to the boys as 'Beau'. He spent most of his time in the staffroom chatting with the English staff, always in my experience the pick of the crop and I'm not sure how we got together; two young bachelors I suppose. I didn't share his indifference to the female sex and he didn't share my interest in sport, but we both enjoyed the theatre and would sally forth from his flat in Clapham in his Renault (not my Hillman for obvious reasons). John had acting experience and theatrical connections and on two occasions I remember going backstage after the performance. After I moved to Birmingham John also worked there for ATV and studied for a Ph.D. at the Shakespeare Institute at the University of Birmingham. He had a very successful career in TV, appropriately fronting the school quiz programme 'Top of the Form' and eventually became Professor and Head of the Drama Department at the University of Wales.

Such were my friends at BGS but my relations with Dr. Langford and Mr. Clark proved less satisfactory. Langford lacked charm and always seemed to be cross and harried. He was for a time chairman of the HMC (Headmasters' Conference, the trade union of leading schools) and also a magistrate, so tended to spend a lot of time out of school. It was soon clear that he had either forgotten the assurance he had given me or that he wasn't prepared to tackle Clark, who liked to think of himself as highly successful at preparing boys for Oxbridge. With Langford frequently absent, it was his deputy, Gerald Cooley, who really managed the school. On first acquaintance I didn't find Cooley a particularly attractive figure, though unquestionably brisk, energetic and efficient. Deputy Heads, of course, are often cast in the role of enforcer and required to do the dirty work. But our relationship steadily acquired warmth and, being no great fan of the obdurate Clark, he warned me that the latter was unlikely to cut me in on any senior work. I took it as a compliment, rather than out of any desire to see me leave, that the drift of his advice was to suggest that I should consider pastures new. I was not too comfortable teaching French, feeling that I had neither the depth nor the techniques needed to spice up my teaching, although I never received any complaints and my performance seemed to satisfy the head of the languages department. I was happy and settled at the school and had things worked out differently I could easily have envisaged a lengthy stay.

By the time my second year at BGS dawned, however, I was becoming restless. The first year of teaching, I would argue, especially for teachers of history, can be very tiring. I felt I had devoted all my energies to the school with little left over for my own intellectual pursuits. I kept in touch with

QMC, mainly through Robert Leslie who was clearly expecting me to focus on a research topic while his wife, Marjorie, who was Principal of an institute in Kingston, hoped to involve me in the launch of an A-level evening class. The juxtaposition of influence at BGS was such that I faced a second year much like the first. At this juncture 'the invisible hand' was about once again to give my career a decisive tweak. Professor Bindoff's many contacts extended to the Midlands where two of his former students were working on research projects and were installed at senior levels in colleges of education. Bill Murphy was working on a Tudor topic, which would result in an MA thesis on the Lord Lieutenancy of Wiltshire in the sixteenth century. He was the senior of two historians at the City of Birmingham College of Education, newly-built and expanding to meet the city's need for teachers and linked to the nearby University of Birmingham's School of Education. Murphy contacted Bindoff to inform him that the college was proposing to offer a small number of Assistant Lectureships enabling young scholars to combine lecturing in their subjects with pursuing their own research. Bindoff contacted me and I sent off for application forms.

My knowledge of Birmingham was limited to short visits to my uncle who lived on the north side. The reputation of the city was of an intensely industrial centre somewhat lacking in cultural facilities and services. To leave my native London was a very considerable step to take and I was no doubt guilty of the condescending attitude of most Londoners to the industrial north. However, my visit for interview came as a pleasant surprise.

I recall arriving at Snow Hill station in the heart of the city and catching a distinctive cream and blue double decker bus to take me to the college in Westbourne Road, Edgbaston. The suburb, 'Birmingham's Belgravia', was impressive, the leafy home of the elite and location of a variety of institutions, among them the University of Birmingham and a number of private schools. The College of Education was housed in relatively new-built premises, praised by Pevsner for its domestic and homely character, surrounded by greenery and with a sports field at rear. Bill Murphy was welcoming and keen to add a fellow QMC-ite to the staff and to please Bindoff in the process. The only other historian at that stage was Mike

Harris, whom I would learn to admire and cherish as a colleague. The college was obviously set on a course of expansion. The Principal, Miss M.M Rigg, was a quite extraordinary woman with a distinct Scottish accent, one of that unmarried inter-war generation of powerful females who went on to become Principals and Matrons armoured in certainties. Miss Rigg was definitely not one to cross and I didn't. She seemed to take a shine to me and decided that there was no reason why I shouldn't become not an assistant but a full lecturer, having had just about enough teaching experience to justify the appointment. It was an offer hard to refuse, above all because it would carry a significant enhancement of salary since most college of education appointees were drawn from senior levels in schools. The downside, of course, was that it was a full-time post and research would have to be pursued in my own time. But a healthy increase in salary as well as an uplift in professional status seemed too good to pass up. I accepted the post, to start in April 1963.

When I was interviewed at Birmingham I had been a single man. When I returned to start work I was no longer single. On 5 April Robin Wyborn and I had been married at Christ Church, Brondersbury. Marriage came on me

City of Birmingham College of Education 1968

like a bolt from the blue. I had certainly not envisaged getting married and I had no material base for doing so. I was still paying off the remnants of my overdraft. But, as so often in life, fate and circumstances had intervened. I had met Robin in November 1962 at a party in Kilburn, at the invitation of an old college friend. Robin was a New Zealander, living in a large house occupied by a group of Australians downstairs and Kiwis upstairs. All were part of that perennial diaspora, a generation of young people brought up on the other side of the world steeped in British culture and determined to experience what was a common *rite de passage*, a year or two of working and travelling in the UK and on the Continent before, in most cases, returning home. Parts of London, their focus, they made their own, Earl's Court tagged Kangaroo Valley and the Overseas Visitors' Club their HQ. Robin had qualified as a teacher in NZ and had initially worked as a supply teacher for Middlesex before applying to become an air hostess with Freddie Laker's independent airline, British United Airways. This suited her fine, she loved travel and flew to places such as Kenya and Cyprus with days off between flights which enabled her to enjoy to the full all the delights that London had to offer and especially the theatre. When we met she was beginning to contemplate returning home and had a ticket on a ship to do so. We met, we danced, we talked and I invited her to come with me on a trip to the south coast next day where I was visiting Dick Wheeler and his family at their holiday cottage at Mudeford. On Monday it was back to work for me while Robin was off to Greece with a friend for a week's holiday. At the end of the week I phoned as I had promised to do and at the weekend we went to see a brilliant production of *Peer Gynt* with the Australian actor Leo McKern in the leading role. (After her death I would find the programme among her things). For the next few weeks we spent all our spare time, which wasn't much, together and the thought of her returning home became unbearable. I proposed and she accepted and at Christmas I was able to introduce her to my family. Most of my family and friends attended our wedding whilst none of hers were able to be present but her flatmates rallied round and organised a reception in their shared house. We honeymooned in Morocco, using airline tickets to Gibraltar and back which Robin somehow wheedled out of BA. When we returned to Roman Rise we packed all our worldly goods into an Austin A35 van which I had spotted for sale near BGS and bought for £75. The risk was all Robin's. She had married a man she had known for less than six months, disappointed her family by not returning home, given up a job she loved and come to live in a city she knew nothing of. Till death us do part!

Postscript

From the spring of 1963 I had ceased to be a Londoner but my links remained strong. My mother lived at 27 Roman Rise until her death. My brother and I bought her house under Margaret Thatcher's legislation and which he modernised. Ian continued to run his shop in Upper Norwood though his margins were shrinking. Ultimately he sold up and retired to Hythe on the Kent coast, which I perceived as south London by the sea. Robin and I made a point of visiting monthly during my mother's lifetime. On Saturday evenings we would either 'go up West' to the theatre or play cards at my uncle's house in Convent Hill. I would usually choose a Saturday when Crystal Palace were at home, my lifelong tribal allegiance. Our connection with London virtually ended with the death of my mother in 1995. My brother and I inherited the house which he was keen to sell, which we did fully furnished. Many of the landmarks in this account of my London life have sadly disappeared and what I most regret is the loss of that nexus of grammar schools which were so familiar to me and which I believed served Londoners well over centuries. A tragic example of state vandalism. After ten years teaching at the Birmingham College of Education I joined the newly-created Birmingham Polytechnic, which became first the University of Central England (UCE) and then Birmingham City University (BCU).

In the later 1970s I also became one of that enthusiastic band of regional tutors underpinning the pioneering work of the Open University and I gained personal satisfaction from once being described by a staff tutor as 'one of the best'. Retirement at the turn of the century gave me more time to research, write, and to lecture in the wider community. Since 2005 I have been honoured by BCU with the title of Visiting Professor and in 2017 I was delighted to be elected President by the Trustees of the Birmingham and Midland Institute, joining a distinguished roll-call dating back to Charles Dickens. My wife died in 2014, deepening my sense of isolation during the dreadful pandemic of 2020-2022 and destroying many of my customary links and activities. This book, my fifth, is a product of 'lockdown'. It is distinctly a view from the engine-room and not from the bridge; more everyman than superman. As an educationalist I look back with nostalgia to the classroom and the lecture theatre, not to the Board Room. I have often noticed that, in old age people's thoughts turn more to their early years. So it is with me. Visions of childhood, youth and early manhood in London come easily to mind. May London, William Dunbar's 'Flower of cities all', survive and prosper and especially S.E.19.